From
I Sit

From Where I Sit

Making My Way with Cerebral Palsy

by Shelley Nixon

SCHOLASTIC INC.
New York Toronto London Auckland Sydney
Mexico City New Delhi Hong Kong

ISBN 0-590-39584-X

12 11 10 9 8 7 6 5 4 3 2   9/9 0 1 2 3 4/0

Printed in the U.S.A.
First Scholastic printing, December 1999

I dedicate this book to all the people who believed in me from the beginning, particularly my family and Donna Jo Napoli. To my friends Agueda, Marleny, Jasmine, and Denise — you are the greatest! And to all my friends in AbleArts — break a leg!

Acknowledgment

I wish to thank Donna Jo Napoli for believing my words have value. Without her assistance as friend and on-site editor, this book would not have been possible. My thanks, also, to Brenda Bowen, my first editor at Scholastic. She granted me the opportunity to tell my story. And to Susan Kitzen, the editor who helped me fine-tune and tighten my manuscript. Her suggestions were invaluable and she was patient.

C. H. Cooley's "looking glass self-concept": Our idea of who we are and what we are is largely determined by the way others relate to us.

Positive self-acceptance is the characteristic that gives you the ability to be yourself, to embrace who you are, and to bring forward . . . your natural strengths.

— A. Edwards and C. Polite, from Children of the Dream

❧ Prologue ❧

I had a friend when I was little . . . Shelley Nick, who I loved very much. Shelley Nick could do lots more than I could. I admired her so much because she could run and jump and climb trees. It was no surprise that she could do more than me; after all, I have cerebral palsy. She didn't. I used to talk to her all the time. I talked to her about my feelings even before I started to write them down. But, unfortunately, she came to a sad end one day. She was hit by a truck. I buried my dear friend in one of my dresser drawers.

I had many imaginary friends in my childhood, but Shelley Nick was my favorite and the only one that I can clearly remember, even though I was only four when she died. But I am getting ahead of myself. . . .

I have lived with cerebral palsy (CP) all my life and, thanks to various programs for disabled people, I've gained many skills. I am definitely making my way in the world, and I am happy. But there's much frustration, too. In fact, being physically dependent is unbelievably frustrating at times. My particular type of CP affects all four limbs of my body, which means I have quadriplegic CP. I have limited use of my hands. I cannot write and typing is slow for me. So I use a voice-recognition computer or I dictate into a tape recorder. I need help in eating and in getting dressed. I can stand with assistance, and I can walk short distances — if someone holds on to me and provides my balance. I do that only around the house, for instance from my bed to the bathroom. I primarily use an electric wheelchair. My speech is slow but people can understand me, if they allow me the time.

I don't think about my limitations on a daily basis. If I did, I believe it might consume me. I wouldn't be able to get anything done. It seems that I fight one of two battles with people who don't know me well. They assume I am mentally disabled since I'm in a wheelchair and/or they assume I can't physically do anything at all. This is not true, of course, and I love to do everything I possibly can for myself. But because of people's attitudes, I feel that I need to work doubly hard to prove myself. Then, once people know me, they discover that I am a hard worker . . . whether at school or at my summer job . . . and the stereotypes disappear. It is just a matter of forcing people to see past my wheelchair. It is an exhausting job.

"What is her name?"

"Can she talk?"

"What does she want?"

People who don't know any better come up to my companions and ask questions like that. I'd like to shout at them, "Ask ME! I'll answer!" Just give me the chance.

For example, once in a restaurant I needed a drink of water, but I didn't have the cup and straw that I usually carry. My dad got a little Dixie cup of water and helped me drink from it. The lady behind the counter rudely asked, "How old is she?" The lady should have waited until I was finished drinking and then asked me.

Another thing that drives me CRAZY is when strangers come up to me and say things like, "My, what a big girl! Aren't you a big girl!" as if I were a baby or mentally disabled. It is condescending.

I sometimes want to scream when I can't do something. I often have to wait for people to do things for me, like take me to the bathroom, dress me, get me a drink, or even turn over a tape in the tape recorder. I cannot imagine how efficient I would feel if I were able to do those things myself. The easiest way to deal with this dependency, I have found, is to ask for what I need and then be infinitely patient while I wait. I usually begin my sentences with, "When you get a chance, would you . . . ?" But the companion of that patience is often hidden frustration.

One way I deal with my frustration is to write. I've written poems and stories since I first went to school by dictating into a tape recorder or to a person. Then someone types what I have dictated. I can say anything I want on paper. Paper can't get angry or impatient. Paper simply absorbs my words and feelings. Writing leaves me with a sense of peace and satisfaction.

When I was asked to write this book, I leaped at the chance. Finally, the chance to answer everything directly . . . to tell my stories to anyone who will listen. My hope is that you will see people who have CP, and people who have other disabilities, through new eyes.

So, listen, please.

✥ Chapter One ✥

"Excuse me, I think I'm in labor!" my mom said.

"No, you're not," said the Lamaze teacher.

My mom was only six and a half months pregnant with me, and it was the first meeting of her Lamaze class, where pregnant women learn techniques that will help them through childbirth. It was way too early for me to be born. But sure enough, my mother's water had broken and her shoes were squishing in it.

"Oh, my God! You better walk across the street to the hospital!"

Mom realized later that was a stupid piece of advice. She should not have been walking anywhere. She should have gotten off her feet immediately. But she was a novice, since I was her first child, so she followed the teacher's directions. At the hospital they put her on an alcohol-drip and elevated her feet. That meant introducing alcohol into Mom's body in a continuous drip through an intravenous needle (IV). The purpose of the alcohol-drip was to keep her muscles relaxed. Since doctors did not have the medicines available today, that was the procedure used in 1977 to delay premature labor.

Somebody called my father, who was in Connecticut. My parents had just sold their house in Houston, Texas, because my dad had been transferred to Connecticut. He was a corporate pilot with Conoco. When the call came about my mom's premature labor, he hopped a "red-eye special" and joined her at the hospital in Houston. My mother stayed on the alcohol-drip and in the elevated bed for three days. But the labor didn't stop. I was born on Saturday, April 23, at 2:03 A.M., two and a half months premature.

I was so sick that the doctors and nurses literally ran with me to the connecting Texas Children's Hospital, where I could get neonatal care. I weighed only three pounds, twelve ounces and was immediately put on a respirator. Among the most serious of my many problems, including collapsed lungs and veins, were patent ductus arteriosis (a heart valve problem) and necrotizing enterocolitis (a portion of my intestines had died).

My mom was discharged from the hospital after three days. She and my dad visited me two or three times daily during the allowed five-minute visiting periods. After twelve days, I was taken off the respirator and oxygen was blown at my face. Then my parents were allowed to hold me, even though I was covered with monitors and wires. Every hour a nurse would prick the heels of my feet with a needle to test the oxygen level in my blood. To this day I still have puckered skin on my heels. In addition to the oxygen and needles, my head was shaved so that an IV could be inserted directly into a vein in my scalp. As a result, I needed a hat to keep my head warm. My parents came up with the idea of cutting off the top of a man's tube sock and sewing one end together. I still have that tiny yellow sock hat. When I look at it now, it seems impossible that I was ever so small. I also developed jaundice, which is a liver problem. I had to wear an eye mask and lie under special lights. My dad glued huge black false eyelashes to my mask, demonstrating the crazy sense of humor that I know and love so well.

After a month, my parents had to vacate our house in Houston and move our belongings to Connecticut. My dad had to begin working there as well. Mom stayed behind with me. She moved into the home of a friend and continued to visit me. Once I was out of intensive care, the allowable visiting periods were much longer. In fact, the nurses encouraged her to spend as much time as possible at the hospital.

At first I was fed through an IV. The doctors asked Mom if she planned to breast-feed me. When she said yes, they told her to buy a breast pump and save the milk, because mother's milk would be especially important for me due to its immunological qualities. Poor Mom. She thought that meant they needed every drop of milk. She pumped every four hours and froze the milk in small plastic bags, carefully labeled. When the hospital staff said that they were ready for her to bring in breast milk, she brought literally two big brown grocery bags full. The staff laughed and then explained to her that I could only take a couple of drops at a time. That was the first of many miscommunications with doctors. My bewildered and embarrassed mother asked if they could use the breast milk for other babies. The staff said, "Probably not." That's too bad because there must have been other sick babies who could have used it.

I was discharged on June 24, 1977, weighing four and a half pounds. The doctors told my parents that I would be fine. Back then it was believed that parents of premature babies should not be cautioned about potential problems because their concern might interfere with the bonding process. My parents remember that one doctor jokingly remarked, "Just put her in the corner, water her a little, and watch her grow." Because they were given so little instruction and help, my parents didn't pick up on my developmental delays until much later. Luckily, today's parents of premature infants are given much more support and guidance.

We flew to our new home in Sherman, Connecticut, on a company plane piloted by my dad. Our dog, a Doberman pinscher named Heidi, was also on board. Heidi panted in my mother's face the whole way because she was so scared. I cried, the dog panted, and it was a bumpy six-hour ride in a small two-engine airplane. No wonder Mom remembers it so well.

Just like most parents of new babies, my parents were happy to get me home. As far as they knew, I had been born prematurely but my difficulties were over. I was just like a normal baby. I was adored. Grandparents and other relatives came to Connecticut to visit us. I was passed from lap to lap. Gammy, my paternal grandmother, had a pet name for me: Lamb chops. My maternal grandmother, Gram, nicknamed me "Doll baby." Gram made a doll for me out of a white sock and some yarn. When I was older I named it Liesl, after my cousin who lived in North Carolina. I slept with that doll for years.

When I first started showing developmental delays, my parents took me to my pediatrician. "Preemies are always slow," the doctor said. "Let's give her more time." But my mom started looking at the charts that show what babies are supposed to do and when. In fact, for everything I was supposed to be doing, Mom added the two and a half months of prematurity. For example, she figured that if I was supposed to sit up at six months, then I should be sitting up at eight and a half months. When the markers she set for me came and passed, she and my dad got frustrated and worried. Finally, after this went on for many months, she took me back to the pediatrician and told him she wanted to take me to Newington Children's Hospital in Hartford, Connecticut. She had been doing some reading. One of the books she had read was *Karen*, the true story of a girl who had cerebral palsy. Mom noticed that Karen's developmental delays were similar to mine. The pediatrician hesitated and said, "Okay, but you might hear the words *cerebral palsy*." Mom was furious that he had not mentioned this before.

I went to Newington Children's Hospital for a three-day evaluation. At the end of all the tests, there was this big meeting. Mom turned to the neurologist and said, "So, does Shelley have cerebral palsy?" The doctor looked at her incredulously. "You mean no one has told you? Of course she does! That was obvious from her complications at birth!" He was seething with anger. The next day was my first birthday.

My parents tell me now that receiving the diagnosis was devastating, but it was also a relief to finally have an explanation for my delays. They were scared because no one could give them answers about what my future would be like. No one could predict whether I would have normal use of my hands or whether I would be able to walk. And, since I was too young to do psychological testing, no professional would even predict whether I was going to be mentally disabled.

Mental retardation is a totally separate diagnosis from cerebral palsy. CP is brain damage caused by head injury or — as in my case — a lack of oxygen before or during birth that affects muscle control and speech. The amount and location of brain damage determines the extent of motor difficulties. Some people have extremely mild CP. Others have it quite severely. People with CP can have normal or above-normal intelligence.

As soon as my parents found out that I had CP, I started going to an Early Intervention class in Danbury, Connecticut. It was for high-risk infants and toddlers who had been referred there by doctors. Today a newborn infant with complications like mine would immediately be registered into a program that would monitor its development at home. Twenty years ago it was different. My parents had to wait until there was a definite diagnosis.

I went to the Early Intervention class one morning a week. The class was sponsored by the Department of Mental Retardation, funded by the State of Connecticut. However, it wasn't just for mentally disabled children. The class was a mixture of physically disabled and mentally disabled children. Various professionals, including occupational therapists (OTs), physical therapists (PTs), speech therapists, and social workers would come into the class and work with the children and their parents. Some of these professionals (particularly the OT, PT, and speech therapists) would do exercises with me. The OT worked on my fine motor skills with my hands. The PT worked on my large muscle skills: crawling, sitting, rolling, etc. And of course, the speech therapist helped me with my speech, which was delayed and unclear. She did this by working on my eating, chewing, sucking (on a straw), and blowing (bubbles). The therapists also gave my mom daily exercise assignments to do with me at home. Combining all of the therapists' instructions, it added up to about three and a half hours a day of exercises — a ridiculous amount. I don't think the people who worked with me were aware of the pressures they were putting on my mother. If she did not get all my exercises done, she always felt guilty and as if she were stunting my growth. If she did get them done, then she felt perhaps she should be doing more.

When I was two years old I joined the preschool class for two mornings a week. In order to get to the class, Mom had to carry me through the halls of the Department of Mental Retardation Adult Program. There were mentally disabled adults of all ages waiting in the halls for their various classes. Even though there were some wonderful teachers and therapists who helped me and my parents immensely, Mom instinctively felt that I wasn't mentally disabled and that if I spent my life being educated with the mentally disabled children in an environment serving only the mentally disabled, I might not reach my full potential. She began to look around for a preschool program for physically disabled preschoolers. She found there were none. So she started one.

She wrote to practically all the pediatricians in northwestern Connecticut and said, "I know you can't give me the names of all your patients with cerebral palsy or any other physical disability, but could you give their parents this letter announcing a meeting?" She held the meeting and met other parents. Through those letters she also found a psychologist who had experience applying for grant money from foundations. The psychologist had also been thinking about starting a school for the physically disabled. She said if my mom would find the kids, then she would write the grant applications and get the money. And they did it!

The preschool program was started in the Stadley Rough Elementary School in Danbury, Connecticut, in 1980. There were seven kids in the class. I was three and a half years old and for the first time I went to school five days a week. Also for the first time, I was in a program housed in a school environment filled with able-bodied children. The program had one teacher, two aides, a physical therapist, an occupational therapist, and a speech therapist. I learned to be away from my mom and dad. The days were filled with stimulation and fun. I began to learn the social skills that able-bodied three-year-olds were learning on playgrounds and in playmates' homes, where I was seldom invited.

Mom tried to solve that dilemma by getting me involved in a play group with other neighborhood kids. One time she made chocolate pudding and put plastic sheeting all over the kitchen floor and up the walls. We played with the pudding and smeared it everywhere. We absolutely had a ball. When we were through playing with the pudding, the kitchen and all of us were a mess. I believe Mom's early efforts to expose me to able-bodied children laid the lifelong foundation for me to be comfortable in situations where I am in the minority.

About this time my parents bought a pontoon boat. We lived on Candlewood Lake. Whenever my dad was home from traveling, we would go out on the lake with other families. There were always about ten little kids on our boat, all of them climbing, running around the boat, and swimming. Since I couldn't do those things independently, I would sit happily in the corner just laughing and having a good time watching all the action. Some of the other adults would go waterskiing, leaving their kids on the boat with me and Mom. We had lots of fun, but I know now that those days on the lake, surrounded by active kids, provided my mom with a constant measurement of what I was not achieving.

When I was four I went to a nondemoninational Bible school. My family is not particularly religious, but this provided me with another chance to socialize with other kids. One day I came home and my mom asked me what I did in school that day — a question I would be asked for years to come. (My father always asks, "How was Sandbox today?" Gramps used to ask him that.) Anyway, I told her we had learned the "Raisin Song."

When she couldn't figure out what I was talking about, I sang with great enthusiasm: "Raisins in the morning, raisins in the evening, raisins at suppertime!" She was still perplexed, until visiting the next day she heard the class singing "Praise Him in the morning, praise Him in the evening, praise Him at suppertime!" It wasn't that there was anything wrong with my hearing. In fact, my hearing has always been excellent. But, like other children, when I heard words I didn't know I reinterpreted them. Years later, when I listened to Beverly Cleary's stories, I was glad to find that Ramona made the same kind of mistake. That "Raisin" story has become a family favorite.

Another story that I am less proud of took place during dinner one evening. When it came up that I would have a day off from school soon for Martin Luther King, Jr., Day, I asked who he was. My parents told me he was a famous African-American. "Was he a waiter?" I asked. My parents were stunned to realize my life was so sheltered in our small New England village that my only concept of an African-American man was as a waiter I had seen in a restaurant. I had never met African-American teachers, doctors, or therapists. We had no African-American neighbors. My parents would not tolerate my innocent misconception. Thankfully, a move to Pennsylvania a few years later changed my view once I started meeting people of different races.

During this time, my dad traveled a lot on business. When he was home he always spent a lot of time making fun things accessible to me. He took me swimming in the lake. He took me on amusement park rides. I loved the speed, spinning, and heights (although they made Dad slightly nauseous). We went ice-skating on the frozen lake, with Dad pushing me in a stroller. He carried me up the endless steps of water slides and put me in his lap as we careened down them. I could always count on Dad to figure out a way for me to try new things — and I still can. Several years later, in fifth grade, I wrote a poem for Father's Day entitled "Best Dad":

Best Dad

(Written in 1989)

Dad is loving,
Though he is shoving
us to bed every night.

Dad is covering,
He is hovering
over us when we are sick.

Dad is funny,
He is sweet as honey.

Dad doesn't let me waste water in the sink,
But I still think
  he is neat.

Dad is handy, because he fixes,
And when he's home he mixes
  our breakfast.

Dad is such a tease,
But sometimes he doesn't let me
  do as I please!

When Dad is gone I miss him,
So I kiss him
  when he comes home!

After each adventure with Dad I always exclaimed, "Again!" He understood me. But others often didn't. I couldn't speak clearly when I was little and only people who knew me well could figure out what I was saying. In fact, when I look at old videotapes of me at that age, I have trouble understanding myself. Teachers had difficulty testing me because often they did not grasp what I meant. Once I had a teacher try to teach me colors by holding up a picture of the color and asking me what it was. Because I couldn't pronounce them clearly and she didn't understand me, she told my mom that I didn't know my colors. My mother knew better. Mom dumped a box of crayons in front of me and asked me to point to certain colors. I had no trouble naming each one.

Another person who could understand my speech was Gammy. When I went on special trips with her, she called it "going on a toot." We went on "toots" for ice cream, out shopping, or out to lunch. It was her way of showing people that they were special to her. I don't know if she took a cue from my parents to include me as much as possible in activities that other kids did or whether it came naturally to her, but I always loved going on "toots."

I also loved going to the movies. It requires no physical skill or dexterity to enjoy the movies. At the first movie my parents ever took me to see, however, I got bored midway and started yelling, "Lights on! Lights on!" In my mind it had lasted long enough. Maybe it was a good thing people had trouble understanding me.

❧ Chapter Two ❧

In the fall of 1981 my mom became pregnant with my brother, John. I was excited until we found out through a sonogram that the baby was a boy. I really wanted a sister. In her third month of pregnancy she almost miscarried and she had to stay in bed for the remainder of the pregnancy. Since she could no longer drive, and my dad was traveling most of the time, a dear family friend, Patty McTiernan, would pick me up each morning and drive me to school. Her mom, Mac, would pick me up in the afternoon and deliver me back home. A friend and neighbor, Peggy Boyd, brought us a big pot of soup each week. My parents hired a young woman, Melissa, to be at our house after school to take care of my mom and me. Each day after school I would sit in bed with Mom and talk and play until dinnertime. I don't believe I ever grasped the real implications of Mom's high-risk pregnancy. No one talked with me about whether or not John would be healthy.

John was born on March 15, 1982, at 8:34 A.M. My mom had gone into labor the night before, so Melissa came to our house and stayed with me. Dad left me a note to read in the morning and then they got a message to me at preschool that my baby brother had arrived. The next day I skipped school and went on a "toot" with my dad. We drove into New York City and went to Tiffany's to buy Mom a pendant in honor of John. We didn't get back to the hospital until late that night. Mom said I arrived giggling and a total mess. We had stopped at my dad's office and the secretaries had spoiled me rotten. I had chocolate all over me and I was wearing most of my lunch. Plus, Dad had dressed me in a fancy summer dress (even though there had been a spring snowstorm that day), used three different colors of barrettes in my hair, and hadn't even made me wear a coat. But I was wearing a *huge* grin.

When my parents brought John home from the hospital at three days old, we never expected him to go back. But he developed jaundice. One morning in that first week my mom noticed that the whites of John's eyes were turning yellow. She

21

probably suspected that he had jaundice because I had developed it in the hospital and she knew the symptoms. My parents called the pediatrician and he said, "Better bring him in." We all gathered in the nursery while Dad packed up a few things and prepared to go back to the hospital. Mom sat in the rocking chair, crying uncontrollably.

I vividly remember sobbing in sympathy. My mother had never cried in front of me before and I was scared. "Don't take him, Daddy! Don't take him!" I pleaded. I finally had the baby that had been growing inside Mom for so long. I didn't want to give him up. And I didn't know if he would ever come back. I was too young to understand that it was what he needed. I consider this my first childhood memory. Up to this point, I have relied upon my parents' recollections about my early years. I truly do remember this scene. John stayed in the hospital for three days. When he came home he was fine and perfectly healthy.

About the same time, I was working with a nice physical therapist named Betsy Utter. She introduced me to the idea of horseback riding as therapy. Maintaining sitting balance on a moving horse requires the use of many muscles. It helped train my muscles to support me in sitting. A friend of Betsy's named Tori knew James Earl Jones, who was the voice of Darth Vader in the movie *Star Wars*. She knew that he owned a horse that was stabled in the area. Tori obtained permission for the three of us to work with his horse, Pancho, each week. I got to ride Darth Vader's horse! Too bad the significance of that was wasted on me because I hadn't seen the movie. Years later, when I finally saw it, I was impressed! Betsy would ride behind me and Tori would lead from the ground. While riding Pancho, Betsy and I would do therapy. I especially loved to trot. Poor Tori would lead Pancho on the trot and would run until she couldn't run anymore. Later, when we moved to Pennsylvania, I got involved in a local horseback riding therapy program. Unfortunately, I didn't enjoy it. The therapist's focus was on therapy, not fun. Therapists need to remember that in dealing with small kids, the kids don't always understand why they need to do the exercises. Therefore, it must be made fun.

In the fall after John was born I began kindergarten at Brookfield Elementary School. Our town, Sherman, had a K–8 school program that was not physically accessible to wheelchairs. Since I was the only physically handicapped child in the town, Sherman could not offer me any programming, so I went to the neighboring town of Brookfield. During the fall I was in a resource room along with other disabled children, where I received special education and therapies. This room had teachers who were trained to give the academic support and physical exercises or positioning needed, along with the special equipment necessary for that physical support. I was mainstreamed into a regular kindergarten classroom in the afternoon for the last half of the school year. Mainstreaming means that disabled children go to school alongside able-bodied children. I spent my mornings in the resource room getting my extra help and then I would join the regular kindergarten class, with an aide to assist me. That year in Brookfield provided me with the invaluable documentation that I would need later in Pennsylvania. It established that I could do the schoolwork expected of me in a mainstreamed program.

I had a wonderful aide at Brookfield, Mary Ann, who I can thank for starting my music box collection. The music box she gave me has a mama cat cleaning the face of her kitten. I love cats and I love music. Unfortunately, I'm allergic to cats, but listening to music is something else I can do that does not require physical dexterity. I have thirty music boxes now.

In November 1982, my dad was transferred to Wilmington, Delaware. DuPont bought Conoco, the company he worked for. If he wanted to keep his job, we had to move the next summer. All of us, except for John, who was a baby, were sad to be leaving Connecticut.

My parents searched Wilmington and southeastern Pennsylvania for a good school district and a house that was wheelchair-accessible. They found the school district but they couldn't find the house. They decided to build one. (We still live in it today.) On our first family trip to the building lot in Pennsylvania, my parents showed it to me and proudly explained, "Shelley, this is where you are going to live!" They were surprised when I didn't show much enthusiasm or ask many questions. When I returned to school in Brookfield, I confided to Mary Ann that we were going to live on an empty lot. I was quite upset. Mary Ann called my parents and figured out what had happened. In turn, my parents carefully explained to me that soon there would be a house on the lot.

About that time I had an electric wheelchair assessment done at Blythedale Children's Hospital in White Plains, New York. The therapists worked with me daily for several weeks to see if I was ready to use an electric wheelchair. After penning one of my therapists in a corner and laughing about it, and then almost driving my chair down a flight of steps without thought of safety, they decided I was too young. Instead, I got a little red manual wheelchair that could be pushed. I needed a chair of some kind because all I had was a great big collapsible stroller. I was getting embarrassed because kids were starting to ask, "Why is she in a baby stroller?" My parents either pushed me in the stroller or carried me in their arms. The little red wheelchair was great because other kids could push it, it went up under tables and desks at school, and it did not look babyish.

Prior to our move, a doctor at Blythedale offhandedly said to my mom, "When are you going to have Shelley's hip surgery done?" Mom asked, "What hip surgery?" She didn't even know I needed it. Once again, due to miscommunication between my parents and my doctors, they learned about my needs in a sudden way. I will never know why people don't explain the whole picture ahead of time. Mom thinks it is because doctors don't like to be the bearers of bad news. The doctors told Mom that if I didn't have my hips operated on soon, they would dislocate. She didn't want to have the surgery in the middle of moving. It would mean weeks in a body cast. We went for a second opinion at the Johns Hopkins Medical Center, and the doctors there said they thought it could be postponed. Then we met with our new orthopedist at Children's Hospital in Philadelphia, Dr. Helen Horstmann. She also said it could be postponed. She recommended that I wear a metal brace at night that had a bar to separate my legs. It was so uncomfortable that I cried almost every night I wore it. The doctor said I would get used to it, but I never did. I couldn't stand being confined in a wheelchair and leg braces all day and then having to put on another brace at night. I felt that I ought to have freedom of movement for at least part of my day. I stopped wearing it and we managed to put off the surgery for two years anyway.

The only other surgeries I had experienced up until then were two eye operations performed at Newington Children's Hospital; one when I was two and one when I was four. One surgery corrected the inner muscles of my eyes, and the other corrected the outer muscles. Around age one, my parents had noticed that my eyes were no longer tracking together all of the time. This muscle problem was a result of my CP. When the eye doctor first examined me he said, "This child has probably been seeing double!" At last my parents understood why I had begun to scream at the sight of strangers. I didn't have the language skills to tell anyone about my scary, distorted vision. The surgeries corrected my tracking, but to this day I sometimes see double when I am tired. The hip surgery was the third of seven surgeries related to CP that I have had in my twenty-one years of life.

When I was little my mom used to introduce me to people by saying, "This is Shelley. She has CP." This was to get me used to the idea that I had CP, as well as to let other people know. One day she noticed that I seemed to be looking around for whatever this "PC" (as I called it) was that I had!

In my head I thought it was a thing, like an object or a belonging. She remembers sitting me down around age three and explaining what cerebral palsy is. She wanted me to feel comfortable saying that I have it. She wanted me to understand it and to understand that I was going to have it for the rest of my life, unless someone comes up with a cure someday. From the beginning she would say things like, "Shelley, you lift your cup like this because you have CP. Other kids lift their cup like this." I cannot imagine how much it must have hurt her to point out those differences. The ironic thing is that Mom didn't even really know all that having CP would mean for me. We have discovered more about it over the course of my life and I'm sure we still have a lot more to learn.

At Johns Hopkins my parents learned from the doctors that there are four different types of CP: spastic, athetoid, ataxic, and mixed. Cerebral palsy resulting from injury at birth is fairly common: Of every 100,000 infants born, approximately 250 are born with some type of CP. Eighty percent of all children with CP have spastic CP. Athetoid CP accounts for another ten percent. The remaining percentage have a combination of types. We were told that I have a combination of "athetoid with underlying spasticity." This means my muscles have too much tone at times. They are unable to relax, so they feel stiff. This is spasticity.

It is confusing because I also have low muscle tone, mostly in my abdomen — and mostly when I am fatigued. This mixed tone helps me in many ways, however. The spasticity gives me a level of support that I use to stand and walk, with help from people. I can give assistance in transferring from my wheelchair. My athetosis causes occasional uncontrolled muscle movements, especially in my hands. I often knock something over or hit people with my hands unintentionally. This is a source of embarrassment, especially in public places. I have spilled things on myself and others countless times. Recently I knocked over the same glass four different times in one afternoon. You can't imagine how bad it feels.

We moved to our new house in Pennsylvania on a Saturday in July 1983. Our station wagon was all packed and just before we pulled away we discovered there were mechanical problems with the car. We had to unpack everything and Dad had to search all over town to find the parts to fix it. We didn't leave until almost midnight and we arrived at the motel in Wilmington, Delaware, around three A.M. When we finally got there, the hotel had lost or canceled our reservations. They ultimately found us a room, but there was no crib for John. Eventually they found a crib but by that time John was no longer sleepy. While the rest of us tried to sleep, John stood in the crib saying, "Mommy, Mommy, Mommy." What a night!

At first we moved into a rental house in Wilmington. The house that we were building in Pennsylvania was not ready. The movers were supposed to meet us at the rental house at eight A.M., which is why we had hurried. My dad got up and went off to meet them. They were not on time and didn't show up with our furniture until midafternon. Meanwhile, my mom was going stir-crazy with us back in the motel room, wondering what was going on, waiting to hear from Dad. She was unhappy, but she was even more unhappy when she finally got to see the rental house. "Filthy" didn't even begin to describe its condition. At one point she found John crawling around with someone's fingernail clipping in his mouth. Yuck. We eventually got the rental house cleaned and we settled in. Dad made frequent trips to Pennsylvania to oversee the building of our house. It was a long, long summer for my parents.

I had a great summer, though! I attended my first summer day camp in Wilmington at Camp Manito, operated by United Cerebral Palsy. Each camper had a personal volunteer. My volunteer was named Heidi, and her thirteen-year-old brother, Eric, also worked there. I fell head over heels in love with Eric. He hung around because of Heidi and he was really sweet to me. I actually asked him to marry me, and he said yes. In his head I was just a cute little six-year-old and he was being nice. But I began to plan a wedding for us at Camp Manito, and everyone went along with this pretend wedding. They thought it was all in fun. Unfortunately, in my mind it was real. I began bugging my mom about the flowers, the invitations, even the honeymoon, and she tried to convince me it was all make-believe. She was unsuccessful and saw it snowballing in my head. She finally called the counselor aside and suggested the "wedding" be called off. I don't think the counselor ever understood how seriously I was involved, but she canceled it. I cried all the way home. My mom said, "Someday you will look back on this and laugh." Between sobs I assured her that would never happen. Of course, she was right. I do laugh about it now.

I loved going to Camp Manito each day. There was swimming, arts and crafts, music, adapted sports, and lots of laughter. I made many friends, some of whom I still see. I am involved in a Wilmington theater group called AbleArts that was founded by a few of those original Camp Manito friends. AbleArts is comprised of twenty-five members, both disabled and able-bodied. I recite my poems and perform in skits, and I am learning to dance in my wheelchair. This involves driving my chair in choreographed dancelike patterns around the floor to the beat of music. We write and direct all of our performances and we are invited to perform at various functions, mostly in Delaware. We have also performed in Pennsylvania, New Jersey, and Virginia. I love it. It is amazing to think that my involvement came about from those early Camp Manito friendships.

❧ Chapter Three ❧

In September 1983, we finally moved into our
new house and I repeated kindergarten at Glenwood Elementary School. I was the only physically disabled child in the school. The people at
Glenwood were inexperienced with a physically
disabled child like me. Physically disabled children
usually went to Old Forge School to participate in
a special program run by the Delaware County Intermediate Unit. Intermediate units are part of
Pennsylvania's public education system. Each unit
serves a specific geographic area and works with
school districts and families to provide children
with special modifications necessary in both cur-
riculum and educational resources.

From my previous school experience in Connecticut, my parents knew I could be successfully mainstreamed. They asked that a mainstream program be established at Glenwood. This took time, so that first year I attended the regular kindergarten class with a personal aide. The people at the school were nice, but they just didn't know what to do with me. At first the principal even called my mom if I needed to go to the bathroom. Fortunately we lived close by and she could run up to the school to take me to the bathroom. She knew that it was going to take some time for people to become comfortable.

I was in the morning Glenwood kindergarten class. When the other kids went home for the day I would go to the Old Forge School and join the kids there. My parents thought it would be helpful for me to spend the afternoon there, receiving therapy and working with the special education teacher. But I hated it. I cried and cried every day. Now that I look back on it, I don't think it was Old Forge that I didn't like. The kids and teachers there were nice. I didn't like that the other Glenwood kids got to go home and I had to go to another school. Eventually my parents and teachers realized it wasn't working so they pulled me out of the Old Forge afternoons. My afternoon teacher at Old Forge was getting frustrated and annoyed with me for continually crying. Ironically, this teacher, Mrs. Wolf, later moved over to the high school mainstream program. She was my high school resource room teacher for four years. We became good friends and still keep in touch.

During that year, an elementary program was busily being planned that would mainstream mentally alert, physically disabled children from Old Forge to Glenwood Elementary School. This was in response to my parents' request, but also in compliance with federal law. The law says that school districts must meet disabled students' needs in the "least restrictive environment." That means mainstreaming as much as possible. The program would serve kids from all over Delaware County, Pennsylvania, since no other elementary schools in the county mainstreamed physically disabled children at that time. Later, the middle school and high school components were added, making it a kindergarten through twelfth grade program. It still exists today in Rose Tree Media School District. It has served hundreds of kids.

In the summer of 1984, when I was seven, I was beginning to get tired of my cerebral palsy. It was finally dawning on me, full force, how many things other kids could do that I couldn't. Plus, John was now two and I was viewing his progress with delight and sadness. I watched *Mr. Roger's*

Neighborhood daily on television and decided to write him a letter. I dictated it to Mom and she wrote it down word for word and then mailed it. Mr. Rogers said on TV that anyone could write a book. That was what made me think about being a writer. Here is my letter:

June 26, 1984

Dear Mr. Rogers:

I wonder if you could come visit me? We would have lots of fun fishing, playing, going to the parks, swinging and talking.

I am Shelley Nixon and I have Cerebral Palsy. I have a brother, John, a mother, Brenda, and a father, Jack. I have CP — John doesn't and Mommy and Daddy don't. I am seven years old. I'll be eight on April 23. John's birthday is March 15 and he will be three. I'm getting an electric wheelchair and I'm going to be in first grade. I go to Glenwood Elementary School. I used to go to a school where there were all handicapped kids. I didn't like it. Glenwood is a regular school and I love it. I have an aide to help me.

I want to meet you in person because I like you and I love you and I wish you could live close to me so I could see you all the time and I could go over to your real house and talk to you and hug you. I guess children write to you all over the United States of America.

If I lived close to you, if you were lonely I could come visit you and cheer you up, because I know John and Jamie don't live with you anymore.

My mommy and daddy said you could come visit us and stay at our house since we couldn't come visit you. Mr. Rogers, I watch your show and I like the way you're speaking and you're understanding. My mommy and daddy don't always understand as well as you do. You are the loveliest man. I wish I could make up a fairy to get rid of my CP. Do you understand that?

You and Mrs. Rogers come up and we will have lots of fun. You can sleep in my bed. I'll take the dolls out. You won't have to sleep in John's room because he cries sometimes. And I'll let you eat beside me.

You said today that I could write a book. So I am going to! You could help me.

Here are my address and phone number. My mommy will put in the directions if you need them. Good-bye. I love you.

> *Shelley Nixon*

I received a personal response from him that I still have. He said he was sorry he couldn't come, but he spoke to me about having cerebral palsy and that he knew it must be hard. I was so proud of his letter. I showed it to everyone.

By the time first grade started, the elementary school mainstream program was in place and I was able to spend a full day at Glenwood. I was so happy! There were six kids, one teacher, Mrs. Mackel, and two aides in the resource room. A few of us were together for the next twelve years, with additional students added to the program along the way. Some of us formed lifelong friendships.

One of my memories from first grade was when I ate ditto paper ink. Yes . . . ditto paper ink. I handled some purple sheets of ditto ink that were on the teacher's desk, and then I tasted the ink. Don't ask me why. I have no idea what was going through my head at the time. But Mom tells me that as a small child I put things in my mouth for years longer than most children do. I couldn't explore things with my hands very well — so I used my mouth, too. I ended up with purple ink all over my face that day. What a ruckus it caused. The school even called the poison control center. For a long time afterward my aides called me "The Purple Gerkel."

I finally got my first electric wheelchair in first grade. I was excited to have the freedom to roam around on my own. My dad remembers I took off immediately and ran the footrests right through a wall. Since I had never crawled or walked, I had no perception of how to navigate. As a baby I would roll on the floor or sit in a chair. Later, I relied upon my little red wheelchair. But I was never able to explore my surroundings like other kids.

Even though I loved my newfound source of freedom, my hand moved so erratically on the joystick that I had trouble driving the chair in the direction I needed to go. My dad found a solution. He put a plastic template over the joystick. It had four slots that would only allow me to push the joystick forward, backward, right, and left. It kept down my erratic movements. After driving with the template for a couple of years, we were able to remove it. By then I had learned how to control my hand.

Soon after getting my wheels, I drove into the kitchen and asked my mom for a dime. She asked me what it was for. I told her I needed it for the New Jersey Turnpike toll. I wasn't kidding, either. One bite of freedom made me want the whole cake! She asked if I knew how far away the turnpike was, and of course I didn't.

Donna Wetzel, who was my physical therapist, helped us make sure the seating system in the wheelchair fit me correctly. I liked Donna, and still do. She is no longer my PT because I no longer do weekly physical therapy. Now Donna is a family friend and consultant to us. When I was little, I got tired of taking PT, so Donna and Mom tried charts to coax me. Every time I was cooperative and worked hard I got a sticker put on the chart. I got to pick the sticker from an assortment. After earning a certain number of stickers I would win a treat, be it an ice-cream cone or a trip to Hershey Park. The exercises I did in PT helped me, but obviously I was too young to realize it then. All I cared about was the fact that many times they hurt. However, I don't know what I would be like today without all that physical therapy.

Physical therapy couldn't solve all my problems, though. At the end of first grade my hip surgery could no longer be postponed. The medical term for the procedure was a derotation osteotomy. My parents waited until school was out for the summer to tell me that the operation had been scheduled. Gram came up from Oklahoma to help care for John. She took John out for a walk while my parents told me about the surgery. I felt scared and started crying. I knew it meant I would need a general anesthesia that would put me to sleep during the operation. I was (and still am) terrified of anesthesia. I had heard in school about a young girl my age dying under anesthesia. Even though general anesthesia is quite commonplace and the probability of someone dying from it is very rare, it is the only part of surgery that scares me. In spite of my irrational fear, I wanted to be an anesthesiologist when I grew up. (A quadriplegic anesthesiologist? Now, that is scary!)

After surgery I was in a body cast for seven weeks. The cast completely covered my feet, legs, and torso. Only my arms, shoulders, and head were free to move. A bar between my legs kept my legs splayed apart. The cast was sticky and hot inside. Whenever I had an itch under the cast, my parents would pound on it.

The doctors had recommended that I spend the seven weeks in the hospital. But my parents felt that would be a long and lonely spell away from home. They rented a hospital bed for my room, along with a small reclining wheelchair that would accommodate my cast. We went out occasionally to the mall or a museum just to get me out of the house.

During those seven weeks I often burst into crying fits out of frustration. I hated that cast. The doctors told my parents afterward that it was "normal and to be expected" from someone confined in a body cast. They thought, *Thanks for telling us now.*

One time I even asked John to get his little blue saw out of his toy tool kit. I asked him to saw off my cast. John sawed as best he could, and I kept saying, "Saw harder, John! Saw harder!" My mom discovered us and gently explained that it wouldn't work.

The doctors also didn't explain to my parents that my body would be atrophied and painfully stiff when the cast was removed. The moment the cast came off, my dad gleefully scooped me up in his arms. I screamed in pain. I had to lie on the floor of the car to ride home. I had to continue to use the reclining wheelchair because I couldn't bend to sit. It took weeks of agonizing therapy to get flexible again. We had not been prepared for any of that. Even with the nicest, most professional doctors and nurses, if we didn't specifically ask for details, they didn't offer them. And, of course, we didn't always know what questions to ask. After all, they were the experts.

Asking John to saw my cast was not the first time I used John's hands as mine. He has been my hands ever since I can remember. When he was a toddler, he couldn't pronounce Shelley. It always came out as Lolly. He would follow me around saying, "Lolly? Want to play, Lolly?" We used to get into all kinds of mischief. I was always the brains behind the ideas and schemes and he would carry them out for me. Once I directed him to scrub our furniture with soap, because I thought the furniture needed to be cleaned. Another time (much to my mother's horror), he mixed, under my direction, all kinds of medicines in the sink, then put my dolls in it. I would tell John how much of each thing to add: "A little more Dimetapp. A little more Tylenol." Then there was the time we put toothpaste on my parents' toilet seat. Or when we played chemist and mixed a dozen kinds of perfumes. Boy, did I stink.

John and I have always been close. His hands are still mine today. Actually, I rely upon a lot of people's hands. But John and I don't get into such mischief anymore. Now I use his hands to fix me drinks, to change the tapes in my tape recorder, or to reach things. And I sometimes use his legs, too. He will run messages for me. And his voice comes in handy. He can yell louder than I can. Because of my CP and my speech problems I am unable to take deep breaths.

While I was writing this book, someone asked me how John feels about having a sister with CP. I honestly don't know. We've never talked about it. But I know he loves me immensely. And the feeling is mutual. I bet that John would be baffled by that question, too. I could ask him. But that would be false, in a sense. We've never had the need on our own to even pose the question.

He is a teenager now. As John has gotten older and has started doing lots of things that I can't do, I've gotten jealous. Watching him makes me wish even more that I didn't have CP. I don't begrudge him the opportunity to do things, though. In fact, I am glad he can ride a bike and drive a car. And that's the truth. I just wish I were able to do it, also. In lots of ways it was definitely easier for me when he was my "baby" brother.

❧ Chapter Four ❧

I started writing stories in first grade when I became discouraged about reading. Reading was hard for me because of problems with my eye muscles. The letters needed to be enlarged and I lost my place easily. I began dictating stories to my teacher and then reading them out loud. As I continued to write stories and read them, I naturally got better at both. I still have problems reading today, however. But I absolutely love listening to books on audiotape. All through school I got novels and textbooks on tape from the Library for the Blind and Physically Challenged. Today I get my college books on tape as well.

Here are two of my early writings:

Memories of My Bathtub Years

(Written in first grade)

Hi! I am an orange bathtub. Today I am going to tell you about memories of my bathtub years in a family of eight children.

I remember when the children would take their baths in me. I would become all sorts of things: ships, trains, and things.

The orange bathroom that I was in became a favorite place to play for the children. The mother would tell them to get out of there, but they wouldn't because they liked me so much! They would use me as a jungle gym. The little two-year-old used the side of me as a horse. I would become a fire truck for Jenny. I would become a house when the children couldn't play outside. The older sister, Julie, would scrub me with a brush. I loved it. The little eight-year-old swam in me.

One day the father caught Joe cracking me and told him to stop it. The twins poked holes in me.

So, this is my story. I am a retired bathtub.

Recipe for the Love Bar

(Written in second grade)

1 teaspoon sugar
8 cups of love
3 packages of kisses
3 bags of hugs
14 ounces of wishes
95 ounces of understanding
4 and 3 cups of happiness milk
A scoop of laughter

Mix all the ingredients with patience. Be careful with the scoop of laughter or it will turn into giggles! Roll the dough into a ball. Drop on a rough surface and roll into a square. Sprinkle lullabies on top. Get all four corners of the square, lift them up, and curl into a bar. Let set for four hours. Put in the glow of love and a ray of sunshine to bake. Cut into squares and serve it whenever you want, with ice cream!

My parents and teachers praised my writing. And strangers did, too. For the first time I could express myself without letting people know I had CP. They could see a representation of my voice and thoughts. They could see my intelligence, playfulness, and creativity. They could know me.

That felt wonderful. And when people stared at me or made fun of me, I knew I had an ability that I could use to fight back.

The first time I was made fun of because of my CP was in second grade. I heard a boy say mean things because I was in a wheelchair. I came home crying. I was sad and for years I hated even the sound of his name. It wasn't until high school, when he was in one of my classes, that I was able to forgive him. He was nice, or at least civil, to me. Being made fun of is not something to be taken lightly. It doesn't help for parents and teachers to say, "Oh, don't worry about it. Just ignore it." It wounds deeply.

My mom remembers a time when I came home and told her about a neighborhood girl saying that people were making up songs about me and singing them on the school bus. Mom says she could have killed the girl. I don't know why that girl felt the need to hurt me. Since I had never done anything to her, and in fact she had been to my house many times, maybe she had low self-esteem and was just striking out at me because I was more vulnerable.

Don't misunderstand. I had friends in elementary school. My peers used to get library books off the shelves for me and help me read them. They did this voluntarily, without the teacher asking. I belonged to a Brownie troop. I was the only disabled child in the troop, and my mother had to be a leader in order for me to belong. She had called the local Girl Scout office to see if there was an existing troop, or a troop that had a leader willing to have me. At that time, locally anyway, Girl Scouts had not quite figured out how to include girls with physical disabilities. There were troops made up entirely of girls with disabilities, but no mixed troops. So Mom became one of three leaders in a new Brownie troop. We went camping and had lots of fun for three years. In general, the girls accepted and included me. It was only occasionally that someone would complain because I couldn't do some of the shared work.

Of course, I also had friends in my resource room where those of us with physical disabilities got extra help and hung out. One of these friends was Jai Sujan. We both lived in the same school district and we used to ride the same school bus. We spent a lot of time together and, as we got older, we grew even closer. Jai escorted me to my proms in high school.

I vividly remember the first time I had enough nerve to express true anger to a friend. I rode the bus with a classmate who would scream as we rounded a certain corner every morning. He had an irrational fear of that corner, just as strong as my irrational fear of general anesthesia. At first I was sympathetic but I finally got fed up with it. I told him I was tired of it and just to stop it. I was astonished when he simply apologized instead of getting mad at me. I was always afraid of making my friends mad. I thought they might abandon me. I was quite compliant.

This was evident when another resource room classmate and I played house each day at noon. She had a milder case of CP than I. She always wanted to be the mother. I did, too, but I didn't have enough guts to stand up to her. So, every day I would just sit there and play the child and let her poke things in my mouth as play food. I would go home and complain to my mom. She would tell me to just say, "Stop it!" But I never had enough courage. Finally, my mom took her aside and told her to stop putting things in my mouth.

I felt the need to be compliant, but occasionally a little bit of rebellion would bubble to the surface. I would be remiss in not telling about the time I cut class. It was a surprise to my teacher because I usually tried to please everyone. One day my teacher was out of the room and I looked around and decided to skip class. No other adults were watching. A friend asked where I was going, and I said, "Nowhere" (the biggest whopper of my life up to that time). I proceeded out the door and took off down the hall. My teacher came back and assumed that I had gone up to my mainstream class for history. My mainstream teacher didn't report my absence because he assumed that I had needed to stay in the resource room for something. I drove all around the school for about an hour and ended up in the teachers' lounge. (There was a Coke machine in there.) A teacher came in and said, "Shelley, are you supposed to be in here?" Since I didn't want to lie to a teacher, I replied, "Umm . . . that's a good question." I was returned to my resource room and I was in major trouble.

As punishment, I was not allowed to drive my wheelchair in the building for a week. Someone would have to push me everywhere. That absolutely crushed me. What made it worse was that when anyone pushed me, they rubbed it in: "Oh, Shelley, I sure wish you hadn't skipped class. This sure makes it difficult for us." My parents knew they could not condone cutting class so they supported the teacher, as far as I knew. Years later, though, they told me that they admired me for having the spunk to do it. My mom did not agree with the teacher's punishment, however. She felt I should have been sent to the principal's office, given after-school detention, or had my recesses taken away just like other kids. No other children were told as a punishment that they couldn't walk around school for a week. My wheelchair was my mobility and Mom didn't think it right that it be taken away from me. I have never cut class since then. I guess I learned my lesson but, like my mom, I don't think the punishment should have been connected to my CP.

Although I loved the freedom of movement that my wheelchair offered, by fourth grade I was becoming frustrated with being confined in it all day. I began having all sorts of problems. For one, I had way too much homework to do every night. I was usually exhausted when I got home from school. Then, not only did I have the regularly assigned homework to do, I usually also had to finish work that I hadn't completed that day in school. And I was becoming more aware of and sensitive to being left out of things. I wrote this story at that time:

The Abandoned Kitten

(Written in fourth grade)

It was December 8, 1989. I still have no idea why my mother didn't like me. She just grabbed the basket that my brothers and sisters and I were born in and she took it to the forest. She put it under a tree. Then she took my brothers and sisters out and told them to follow her home. But she left me there! I was cold and hungry. And I almost got eaten up by a porcupine!

I stayed there until the twenty-second of December. Much to a black mother bear's dismay, I nursed with her cubs to stay alive. In the middle of the night I felt something grip around me! I opened my eyes to see a wild ferret!

He carried me far away to a hole where he had his home.

"Violet, I found the perfect baby for us to keep and treasure for the rest of our lives," said the ferret to his wife. Oh, yea! I thought in delight. I didn't even care if I had to live my kittenhood in a hole in the ground. I knew I would be nice and warm, but most importantly I knew I would have a family to love me even if they were not my biological family!

They decided to name me "Christmas" since I came right before the holiday. I spent my kittenhood with my adopted ferret family. I am a cat now and I no longer live in the hole. I have a cat wife and our own kittens. I am still thankful for my ferret family. I keep in touch with them and go back to visit.

The moral of this story is: Never refuse to be part of a family, or to be friends with someone just because they are different than you.

The magnitude of my disability, and its permanence, was finally dawning on me. I would start crying over something and I literally would not be able to stop. The crying would elevate to screaming, which would last for hours. I would wail at the top of my lungs. Mom said I sounded like an injured animal. I basically stopped communicating my feelings to my family, teachers, and friends. Even writing only helped a little.

My parents took me to a psychologist to work through some of my frustrations. Her name was Regina, and I liked her a lot. I saw her weekly and she helped me over the next five years. Regina helped my parents, too. Mom learned that some of her responses, whenever I did open up about my feelings, were not what I wanted to hear. For example, when I would talk about how I felt about having CP, she might say, "Just be grateful your CP is not worse," or "Be grateful that you are not mentally disabled." Regina was able to explain to Mom that I already knew that on a logical level, but it didn't help me on an emotional level. What I wanted to hear was, "I know it's tough that you have CP. I know it must make it even tougher to watch your friends do things you can't." In other words, I just wanted someone to listen and empathize. I knew all the logical stuff and I wasn't looking for a way to make it all better. Regina helped me understand that parents generally want to make things all better for their children and it hurts when they can't. I don't cry easily now and it has to be something pretty big to make me cry.

It is probably apparent by now that I am a "pleaser." I dislike — no, loathe and despise — conflict. It doesn't even have to be about me. It doesn't even have to be big or loud. When there is conflict around me, I usually go into extension (my whole body becomes stiff) and practically stand up in my chair and look wild-eyed at the people involved. My family has described this to me but I am completely unaware of it. They say I look like a deer caught in headlights. Regina explained to me and my family that physical dependency increases the tendency to avoid conflict at all costs. In other words, you don't want to make someone mad if you are dependent upon them. They might decide not to help you, and then where would you be?

While writing this book, I discovered an article I wrote for my middle school newspaper, and I have included it here. It made it clear to me how very much I tried to be cooperative and to hide any anger I felt. As you will see, several times I mention being grateful for people's acceptance and patience. Once again, my words on paper reflected the real me, while my actions reflected whatever I felt it took to navigate society.

A Day in the Mainstream

Handicapped program offers many exciting challenges

(Written in sixth grade)

I can guarantee you that being surrounded by a hall full of kids and trying not to run into them with my wheelchair is a difficult feat! Nobody wants tire tracks up their back! I am sure apologetic when it happens, but after all, this chair didn't come with a driver's license! But most everybody is nice about it, and I'm grateful for that.

The teachers in Springton Lake accept me and they are patient. They look past my wheelchair and see the part of my body that is capable: my brain. The teachers don't make me feel guilty when I can't do something in class that other kids can do. Maybe they understand that my hands don't always cooperate. And, boy, is that frustrating for me! They don't act like they feel sorry for me, either, and I am glad.

I'm grateful to students who help me out, too. Even my friends in the Resource Room. I get tired sometimes of having to ask for assistance but I must do it, otherwise I couldn't get the things I need. I know I am given special privileges sometimes. But it's certainly not in homework! But that's OK.

This program in Rose Tree Media School District is important to me because, otherwise, I would have to go to a school for only the handicapped. By getting to go to Glenwood and Springton Lake, I have met friends I wouldn't have met otherwise.

I can't say that I enjoy being handicapped, but I *can* say that I enjoy the handicapped program at Rose Tree Media.

In retrospect, I believe mainstreaming me into regular classrooms gave me the survival skills to make my way in the world. I learned what was required of me to bridge the gap between the able-bodied and disabled. I became perceptive in recognizing friendship over pity. Sometimes I endured hurtful social lessons, but they only made me stronger in the end.

❧ Chapter Five ❧

Pond View Lane, the street I live on, is relatively quiet. There are only five houses on it and it has little traffic. That is one reason my parents chose it. When I was little I would pull my neighborhood friends up and down the street, with them hanging on the back of my electric wheelchair and wearing roller skates. Once John tied his Big Wheel on a long rope to the back of my chair and I pulled him down the street. That was fun.

One day I asked Mom if I could drive to the stop sign. My mom thought I meant the stop sign at the end of Pond View Lane. But there is another stop sign at the entrance to our neighborhood, down a hill about half a mile away. Mom said yes, and I was halfway down the hill when my brother caught me by the ponytail.

When John was little, I was a big sister who spoiled him rotten. If he wanted something of mine, no matter what it was, I would always say yes. That drove my parents crazy because they were trying to teach him that he couldn't always have his way. But I was doing everything in my power to please him, probably to keep him willing to help me. I don't do that anymore. I am able to say no to him now.

The first time I was totally away from John was in the summer of 1988. I was eleven and I was adamant that I was going away to an overnight summer camp. Mom had asked me the previous summer if I wanted to go and I had said no. By the time I was eleven, I was definitely ready for my independence. When I was dropped off, I didn't even look back or cry. I didn't like the camp much, but I didn't let that stop me from having fun. The next summer I went to a different camp and liked it much better. I attended it for three summers. Each summer I eagerly looked forward to leaving my family and being on my own. During my last summer at that particular camp, I grew quite attached to one of the counselors and her boyfriend, who was also a counselor. In fact, I asked them to become my backup legal guardians. I envisioned

John and me living with them. What fun! I am amazed at the intense friendship and feelings that arise between campers and counselors at summer camp. I still try to attend a week of overnight camp each summer. Now, of course, I go to a camp for adults, operated by a rehabilitation hospital. I love meeting new people. It is like taking a vacation.

Anyway, after that first summer of enjoying a new level of independence from my family, I came back to a new resource room teacher for my fifth-grade year. All of my teachers had been nice and my new one, Mrs. Matus, was no different. But unlike my former teachers, Mrs. Matus gave less nightly homework. A bit of relief in that area not only helped with my fatigue, but it also helped with a problem that had been growing between my mom and me.

Throughout my school years my mom has been the one to help me with homework. I have no recollection of how this arrangement went prior to third grade. But I specifically remember that when I was learning the multiplication tables we began to have arguments. Our homework sessions were difficult through the rest of my grades. It had nothing to do with what I was studying. I just did-n't want to do homework with my mother. Since I can't write, and usually the print in books and classroom papers is too small for me to see clearly, she acted as my scribe: She read and wrote for me. Because of this, we had to do homework when it was most convenient for her, not necessarily when I wanted to. I usually started out resentful.

That fifth-grade year, not only did my resentment go down because of the temporary reduction in homework, but two really special things happened. First, my grandmother moved up to Pennsylvania from Oklahoma. Gram moved partly because John and I had never had the experience of living around any extended family. We were thrilled to have her nearby. Every time her foot hit our threshold, John would run to her and I would bounce up and down in my chair. We loved going to her house, too. She always had candy in a dish and never said no when we asked for some. For the first time we had family around for holiday dinners or to attend our special school functions. Our grandparents, aunts, uncles, and cousins were scattered all over the country. Before Gram moved we only saw our grandparents about once a year. We saw our cousins even less often. I always envied kids who had cousins to play with. I knew I could count on family members to accept me unconditionally and to include me in everything.

Second, we got our dog Prince. John had wanted a dog for years and Dad had been saying, "No, no, no. . . ." But we kept hammering on the subject and one day Dad said, "Okay! Do what you want!" We thought that meant he had finally agreed. The next time he was out of town my mom took John and me to the animal shelter. I was in my portable wheelchair and when Mom pushed me into the area where the cages were I immediately said, "I want *that* one!" I pointed at a six-month-old black Labrador-mix puppy in a cage behind the door. His name was Bear. We also spotted a beautiful golden retriever puppy. We asked if we could see both dogs in the outside yard. The golden retriever jumped all over the place. When Bear came out in the yard, he walked over to me and gently laid his head on my shoulder. I knew right away he was the one. We wanted a dog that would be calm around my electric wheelchair. Bear was only one day away from being put to sleep. We renamed him Prince and brought him home. When Dad returned from his business trip, he was not happy about Prince. He had not truly meant it was okay. Prince was especially drawn to Dad, though, and eventually Dad couldn't resist him. They became fast friends. They went for walks together each night and worked in the yard together.

Prince gave us his unconditional love. He made it his personal responsibility to clean bits of food from the side of my wheelchair each day. He lived to be nine years old. We had to put him to sleep when he developed a cancerous tumor in his nose.

We loved him enormously and that was a dreadful day. Dad and John held Prince while he was put to sleep. I didn't want to be in the room. I remember the last thing I said to Prince before I left the veterinarian's office was, "Good-bye. I am sorry I couldn't walk you or run with you or do things like that!" I began to sob, saying, "I HATE MY CP." Those regrets and feelings surfaced so quickly that it surprised even me. My CP had nudged its way into my deepest grief.

I don't know exactly when I started writing as a catharsis for my feelings. As I continued my writing, people would read my stories and they liked them. I switched from writing stories to poetry in middle school. Here is one:

Hurry

(Written in sixth grade)

Hurry! Says the morning,
It's time to wake up!

Hurry! Says the aide,
You have to eat faster!

Hurry! Says the mother,
Quickly say the Spanish words!

Hurry! Says the father,
Hurriedly drink your milk!

Slowly! Says my hand,
While driving my wheelchair.

❧ Chapter Six ❧

In seventh grade I won my first writing award:
the Young Authors Project of Delaware County,
sponsored by the Delaware County Intermediate
Unit. This is an annual contest for young writers,
grades one through eight. My language arts
teacher actually had to talk the organizers of the
contest into accepting my essay, "It's Only Thunder." According to their rules, they wouldn't accept any dictated material. I cannot write and, at
that time, I did not have my voice-recognition
computer program. I vividly remember overhear-
ing my language arts teacher tell my resource
room teacher that the organizers would not accept
my work. I was so used to being left out of things
that I didn't think much about it. Thankfully, my

teacher persevered on my behalf. What makes it especially ironic is that the Delaware County Intermediate Unit, the sponsors of the contest, also ran my school program for the physically disabled. You would think that they would have been the last people to discriminate.

I won the award the next year as well for "Ice Dreams." Both years that I won, the awards ceremony was held in an auditorium that had a stage inaccessible to wheelchairs. When my name was called, my dad had to lift me up on the stage, wheelchair and all. It was a good thing I was still small. Here are those two writings:

It's Only Thunder

(Written in seventh grade)

Last night my family and I were sitting around the TV watching the news about the beginning of Operation Desert Storm. Just as they were announcing possible missile launches by the Iraqis, a HUGE clap of thunder crashed outside! My eight-year-old brother's whole body stiffened and his eyes got enormous. He turned to my dad and asked if we were being attacked. My father answered, "It's only thunder."

It was then I started wondering: Since distance

has no meaning to my little brother and he doesn't really understand that it is half a world away, what would it be like to be an Iraqi child now? What would it be like to be in a place where your parents couldn't say, "It's half a world away," or "It's only thunder"?

I imagined an Iraqi family waking up to hear the sounds of bombing and feeling the shaking of their house. An Iraqi little brother must have been scared to death! His family could see fire out the windows, and probably smell it, too. They could hear sirens blowing. The Iraqi child must have gotten terrified, just like my brother, but his parents couldn't comfort him with "It's only thunder." I couldn't even imagine what it would be like to wonder if, at any moment, you would be blown off the face of the earth. My dad turned off the TV. The Iraqi family couldn't turn off the war.

My little brother got ready for bed. When he got into bed, he was afraid to turn over, because he was afraid that a "bad" Iraqi soldier might be in his room. I wondered what it would be like for an Iraqi child to be afraid of a "bad" U.S. soldier in his room. If we believe our U.S. soldiers are the good guys, do you suppose that the Iraqis feel the same about their soldiers? In the eyes of the children, who are the good guys?

If I had a lucky penny to wish on today, I would wish that Saddam Hussein would be locked up in jail and that this war would end. And, as my social studies teacher said, "This would be the last war of its kind." All parents should be able to say, "It's only thunder."

Ice Dreams

(Written in eighth grade)

I fly through the cold air as lightly as a snowflake. Just before I fall on the ice, my partner catches me and we swirl neatly on our skates.

Am I really ice-skating? No. In real life I am a fourteen-year-old girl with quadriplegic cerebral palsy. I use a wheelchair. I only skate in my mind. I have had these dreams ever since I was a little girl. My imagination allows me to outrun my limitations. To enter my world of freedom I simply have to close my eyes:

The ice under my skates feels smooth as I glide over its shining surface. I feel like I have wings! Taking deep breaths and long strides, I start my strenuous routine. My muscles remind me they are still sore from many hours of practice yesterday. I stretch them out over and over again, with my eyes on the time. Today I will skate to the music "Wendy" and "He's Got a Ticket to Ride." My routine makes me feel fanciful. I am practicing for my big show tomorrow. When I skate, I feel every inch of my height. I am straight and tall, like a willow tree.

I open my eyes. I am back in my wheelchair. I don't want to leave the ice-skater that I am in my dream, but I can be fanciful in the real world, too. I do that by writing. I receive comfort from the fact that I can always visit the Shelley Nixon who isn't handicapped and *be* that person, for a while, in my mind's eye.

"Ice Dreams" is currently a part of a study unit on disabilities at my old middle school. Mrs. McBreen, the middle school resource room teacher, uses it to help able-bodied students understand the frustrations and feelings of disabled students. She tries to help them see, through "my mind's eye," that we have yearnings. And escapes. Probably just like them. And so, maybe we aren't so very different after all.

My middle school years were rough due to illness and death in my family. Gammy, my paternal grandmother, who lived in Louisiana, was diagnosed with lung cancer and died six weeks later. Prior to that she had been taking care of Gramps, who had pancreatic cancer. Ironically, he was doing better when she was diagnosed. I remember the day she died. It was November 15, 1989. It was a school morning, and I was dressed and eating breakfast at the kitchen table. The phone rang and Dad answered it. After a conversation with my grandparents' housekeeper, he hung up, turned to us, and said, "She died." Mom jumped up and put her arms around him and I immediately started crying. I was so upset. It was the first time someone I knew and loved had died. I went back to my room and Dad came in to see if I was okay. I said, "Dad, I'm sorry." I was sorry because I thought it was my fault Gammy had died. I had wished her dead two days earlier. She was in a lot of pain and I had wished her to be out of her misery. I didn't realize that you couldn't wish something like that and have it happen.

Wishing Gammy dead was a wish that came true when I really didn't want it to. I had made many wishes over the years. I had wished for a pill or a fairy that would cure my CP. I had wished that my learning disabilities and visual problems would go away. I had wished for a boyfriend. I had wished to be invited to dance parties and girls' slumber parties. I had wished my allergies to cats would disappear. None of those good wishes came true. But this bad wish had. Was a wish about death more magical than a wish that I could walk? It was pretty scary.

Dad flew down to Louisiana for Gammy's funeral. The rest of us stayed at home. Mom, John, and I spent a lot of time over the next few days talking about Gammy and her life. I remembered that when I was five and she was visiting us I had said, "Gammy, let's have a rock a little, sing a little, talk a little." She asked, "What's that?" Well, it was just exactly what it sounded like. It became a standard thing between us when she visited. She knew dozens of songs from her childhood. They always sent me into giggles. I heard funny stories about my dad as a little boy. And, of course, she listened to me. I miss those special times with her.

While Dad was away at the funeral I proudly brought home my first middle school report card. I had made the honor roll. In elementary school there was no honor roll. So this was my first chance to face that challenge — and I met it. I was looking forward to praise. Instead, in her grief, Mom didn't even acknowledge it. I felt cheated even though I was so sad over Gammy's death, too. I finally said something to Mom. She apologized but it still hurt. Losing Gammy hurt more, though.

It is a tradition in my dad's family to bury people sort of like the Egyptians do. That is, they bury their ashes with special things that they liked and treasured here on earth. We have a private cemetery in Louisiana so the family members can do whatever is most meaningful. They buried Gammy's ashes in a huge bouquet of flowers.

After Gammy's funeral, Dad invited Gramps to come back to our house for a visit. Thanksgiving was drawing near and my parents thought he might feel better being with us on the holiday. Then the plan was that he would fly down to North Carolina to Aunt Penny's house for the Christmas holidays. However, once Gramps got here we realized how sick he was. He was too sick to go to Penny's for Christmas. Instead, the whole Nixon clan gathered at our house for Christmas to be with him.

Gramps lived with us for about four months. In March we had to put him in an assisted living/nursing home because he just kept getting sicker and sicker.

The summer after Gammy died, my dad found a lump in his neck while shaving. For a while he wouldn't see the doctor about it, but Mom finally convinced him to go. We had planned a family vacation to Duck, North Carolina, but the doctors wanted to do a biopsy quickly. They weren't sure if it was cancerous. Mom told us that we were going to have to cancel our vacation because Dad needed surgery. I started crying because I wanted to go to the beach. Now, though, looking back on it, I think I was really crying because I was sure that something was wrong. I was scared.

Arrangements were made for John and me to stay at friends' houses during the surgery. I went to my friend Jai's house and John went to our neighbors', the Christiansens. I was terrified. Unfortunately, I knew the exact time scheduled for his operation. I pestered Jai all day asking what time it was. I kept pressing the button on my watch to hear the time. At one point Jai said, "You're scared, aren't you?" I replied, "Yes, I am." He tried to keep me occupied with music or TV. Jai's mom brought me home that evening. Gram told me that the surgeon had to remove the entire muscle in one side of Dad's neck. (The technical term for that excised muscle is sternomastoid.) What was supposed to be an outpatient day surgery turned into an entirely different scenario. He had head and neck cancer.

Mom pulled John and me aside separately and told us the news. I began to cry. Based upon my two recent experiences with my grandparents' cancers, I thought that meant he would die. Dad came home and took several weeks of radiation treatment. (Nine years have passed and he is now declared to be cancer-free.)

Gramps was in the nursing home during my dad's summer of cancer treatment. He fell and broke his hip in the fall, and then his final decline was unstoppable. He died on the morning of December 4, 1990. When my mom told me that afternoon, I immediately demanded to know why I hadn't been pulled out of school. "There was no point," she said. "But I could have done something!" I protested. "Like what?" she replied. "There was nothing anyone could have done. He was too sick." I just felt so helpless surrounded by death and sickness.

I insisted on seeing Gramps the Saturday before he died. It was important to me. John didn't want to go because he just didn't want to see Gramps so sick. I don't remember how he looked, but there is one thing I do recall: Like Gammy's "rock a little, sing a little, talk a little," Gramps and I had our own special game that he called "chin-chopper." It was sort of silly, but I loved it. He would put his hand under my chin and quickly move my head up and down saying, "Chin-chopper, chin-chopper, chin-chopper." I would break into giggles. I had asked him to do it one last time. I can still remember how frail and weak his hand felt beneath my chin.

Two days after Gramps's death I wrote this essay in school:

My Summer Lesson:
Don't Take Someone for Granted

(Written in seventh grade)

Last summer I had an experience that I will never forget for as long as I live. It started in May.

My father felt this lump in the left side of his neck. After seeing several doctors, he had two surgeries. In the second surgery they removed most of the neck muscle on the left side. They discovered he had cancer. He came home with thirty-four staples in his neck. He was weak. He often had to be excused from the table because he was so weak. He had eight weeks of radiation every day, which made sores in his mouth and throat. He lost his sense of taste. He could only eat cream soup for the whole time.

As for me, before I found out that he had cancer he told me our summer vacation might have to be canceled. I knew it was something serious, even though my parents didn't act as concerned. I remember on the night after my dad's surgery, I was crying and I said to my mother, "I shouldn't be doing this," because my younger brother, John, wasn't crying. I felt I was acting younger than he was, and I should have been more mature. My parents were very good about not hiding things from us. We could ask any questions. It was okay to cry. A couple of mornings after his surgery my mother told me he had cancer. Since my grandmother had died from cancer only six months earlier, I was frightened! Also, my grandfather had cancer!

When my dad came home I couldn't look at him for a long time afterward. In fact, I still have some trouble. The scar is barely noticeable now and he isn't weak. But when I look at him I can't help but wonder, "Is it going to come back and kill him?" That thought is almost unbearable to me. The reason I couldn't look at him when he came home from the hospital was because I was almost comatose with fear that he was going to die. He looked awful. He looks great now and acts like my old dad but, nevertheless, that fear is still there.

During the summer our family was affected in a number of ways. Our vacations were canceled. My little brother went to eight weeks of day camp, when he normally goes for six weeks, because my parents thought it would be no fun for him to be around the house during radiation. I had my regular camp schedule. In spite of it all, my dad tried hard to act normal. My mother was under a lot of stress. John was afraid that Dad was dying, but he tried to act like he wasn't afraid. We still had our grandfather to take care of, too.

My grandfather died this week from his cancer. Before all of this I didn't know much about cancer. I know a lot now and I don't think I want to make any new friends who have cancer, because I might get attached to them and they might die. I am tired of death. And I don't trust doctors' predictions on death, either! They were wrong about both of my grandparents. My grandfather's death has made me feel more tired and afraid. Don't ask me why, because I don't know. I just do.

My dad is back at work now. We laugh more and we are getting ready for Christmas. Everything is okay now, I guess. But I guess I'll always wonder if there will be another Christmas with my dad.

❧ Chapter Seven ❧

Gramps's funeral, like Gammy's, was held quickly. No big gatherings, no big ceremonies. Dad took Gramps's ashes to Louisiana and the rest of us stayed behind. We were totally saturated and exhausted with emotions after the year of stress. We had already said our good-byes to Gramps. His ashes were buried in a model of a wooden boat that he had built many, many years before.

Little did I know that after watching three loved ones battle cancer in a year and a half, with my dad the only victor, I would have to watch another family member face the same fate. Nine months after Dad completed his radiation treatment and five months after Gramps's death, Dad's sister, Penny, was diagnosed with brain cancer: astrocytoma. They operated immediately but it had already spread to the point that the prognosis was poor. She would be the third member of the Nixon family to die of cancer in three years.

I remember going to see her the summer after her diagnosis. Aunt Penny was clearly sick from her cancer. We all knew she was terminally ill, and she was brave and up-front about it. At one point she was talking about getting her affairs in order, what she was going to give to whom, etc. I looked up at her with tears in my eyes. She said, "Shelley, do we need to talk?" For once in my life, I did not say, "No. Nothing's wrong." I blurted out, "Aunt Penny, why are you talking about this as if it is going to happen tomorrow?" She grinned and replied, "Shelley, you never know. I could die tomorrow. No one knows when they are going to die. I could get hit by a truck tomorrow."

There is another specific thing I remember about that visit with her. I happened to comment that I liked her fish-shaped earrings. She smiled, reached up and removed them, and said, "You like them? Here. You can have them." Then she told me a story about when her aunt did the same thing for her when she was a young girl. I cherish those earrings.

Sadly, Aunt Penny's last month was spent in bed, totally incapacitated. I had sent her a special stuffed cat, since she loved cats so. The stuffed cat meant a lot to me, and it was all I had to offer her for comfort. She wrote a wonderful letter to thank me and told me the stuffed cat sat on her bed all the time. That was the last letter I ever got from her.

On October 15, 1991, I went into our den and asked my dad if Aunt Penny had died yet. I asked without any premonition or inkling that it may have happened. I just knew that it could be any day. Dad answered, "We were going to tell you and John together, tonight at dinner. She died at three-fifteen this afternoon." It was the day after her fifty-second birthday. I started crying. I felt such mixed emotions. I was happy to see her out of pain, but I was sad to lose her.

We all went to her funeral in Louisiana. We felt we needed the closure. In keeping with family tradition, Aunt Penny's ashes were buried in a basket surrounded by her favorite things: her walking sneakers, her reading glasses, her favorite book. At the last moment I added the special stuffed cat. I wrote this poem about Aunt Penny as a school assignment the next year:

In the Prime of Her Life

(Written in ninth grade)

She sat in her kitchen,
Early morning sunlight streamed on the back of
    her half-bald head.
The other half of her head was covered with
    patches of light brown hair, neatly scattered
    all over.
A pink scar divided her scalp.

The plate of peach pie and ice cream sat in her
    right hand.
As she stabbed the pie with her left, the fork
    dropped.
Her hand shook as she slowly picked it up from
    the table
    and brought it to her mouth.
A triumphant and defiant grin flashed across her
    face.

She is my Aunt Penny.
She is dying,
Pie for breakfast?
Why not?

"Astro Cytoma."
A pretty name

For something so horrible.
In the prime of her life.
Its fingers grasping through her brain relentlessly.

Taking away functions.
Her personality.
Her future.
Her life.

Slow. Painful. A tragedy.
She didn't deserve it.
And she knew it.
And she cried.
But her spunk!

"No more green tomatoes or cheap wine. Life is
    too short."

Our lesson from Aunt Penny.

We buried Aunt Penny like an Egyptian,
    with special things all around her.
Her ashes in the family's favorite picnic basket.
(She loved early morning breakfast picnics.)
Her battered, worn sneakers.
(For her afternoon walks, around the clouds
    now.)
Her childhood *Winnie-the-Pooh* book.
(She read it to her kids.)

Her reading glasses.
(She can't read up there without them.)
A tape of classical music. Some pistachio nuts.
And on top . . . my stuffed cat.
(The one I sent to comfort her.)
Then we sang "Amazing Grace."
And she was buried with grace.

Even though there was a lot of sadness, death, and illness during my middle school years, I wasn't totally unhappy. Mrs. McBreen, my resource room teacher, was wonderfully supportive. I had great mainstream teachers, too. I found I was still able to take joy in so many things. Here are two poems from eighth grade.

Winter

Snowflakes falling to the ground.
Icy winds swirling round and round.
Frozen ponds and black finger branches.
No more allergies!

Christmas and "snow days," a wonderful
    treat!
Hot chocolate, open fires and toasty feet.
And . . . no more allergies!

Ice-skating and sledding.
Snow ice cream to eat.
Clouds of breath in the air whenever you
speak.
And — best of all — no more allergies!

I love winter!

If I could, I would . . .

ice-skate
walk by myself
bring Aunt Penny back
eliminate cerebral palsy
eliminate poverty
install "Save the Children" in every school across
    the nation
get rid of red beans and rice
take away the death part of muscular dystrophy
    and cancer
change all the music in the country to
    "oldies"
outlaw egg salad
put a cat in every home
eliminate allergies
become a famous author
become the first female President of the U.S.
serve restaurant food for school lunches, instead
    of school food
change the voting age to 14

make all medicines taste like chocolate
declare every Tuesday a national holiday so
      schools would close
make students the boss for one day a school year,
      so teachers would have to mind them!
stop air pollution
make Christmas last eight days

I had a lot of friends in those years, especially in the resource room. One day in eighth grade I expressed my fears about an impending surgery. Instead of helping me calm down and feel better about it, my friends began telling me their own hospital horror stories. Jimmy, whose life would be tragically shortened due to muscular dystrophy, jumped to my defense. "Hey, guys! Get off her back! She is scared! She doesn't need to hear how horrible it was for you!" I was lucky to have a friend like him.

The surgery I needed was a hamstring and adductor release. Hamstrings are muscles down the back of the thighs. Adductors are muscles in the upper thigh groin area that assist in the motion of spreading your legs apart. A "release" is a way to surgically lengthen and stretch those muscles. Continual sitting in a wheelchair tends to shorten them. They had been released once before, at the time of my hip surgery, but now they needed to be

released again. I wrote this poem four days before
the surgery:

(Written in February 1992)

Surgery is a risk you take
When you want to make the pain go away.
But will it really make it go? Is it so?
Is it really safe?
Or, am I putting myself in danger whenever
    I go?

What if something goes wrong,
    and I might never be able to sing a song?
And, while you are asleep, anything can happen
    to you.
Since I won't be under local,
And I won't be vocal,
What might happen to me?

Are doctors really that safe?
Can I trust their skill?
If I am asleep and my parents aren't there to
    watch over me,
What's to keep them from making a mistake?

And, I mean, a HUGE mistake!
There are so many patients coming in and
    out —

What if they mix me up with someone who needs
   their arms worked on?

I am apprehensive. I wouldn't call it scared.
I am looking forward to getting it over with.

I still had my fear of anesthesia, but I chose not
to take the presurgery sedative. It was important
to me to be wheeled into the operating room wide-
awake. After surgery I wore soft casts with Velcro
straps on both legs. I had leg extenders on the
front of my wheelchair and I returned to school
fairly quickly.

❧ Chapter Eight ❧

As I entered high school I expected that my family's cycle of illness and death would continue: one per year. Fortunately, it didn't. My family was safe.

In May 1993, I wrote this poem as an English class pantoum assignment (pantoum is a type of poem with a particular scheme of repeating lines):

Portrait of My Dad

(Written in ninth grade)

My dad in his hammock, sleeping on his back.
Out in nature with his arm slung over his face.

Just swinging in the breeze.
With the sun shining down.

Out in nature with his arm slung over his face.
His shirt sticking to his back.
With the sun shining down.
Legs stretched out in blue jeans.

His shirt sticking to his back.
Sleeping peacefully without a stir.
Legs stretched out in blue jeans.
Birds twittering overhead in the trees.

Sleeping peacefully without a stir.
His classical music playing softly.
Birds twittering overhead in the trees.
He looks so serene lying there.

In ninth grade I fell in love with a boy in my class who was awfully nice to me. As far as he was concerned, we were just friends, but I was truly "in love." I began writing real lovey letters to him on my computer in the resource room. These were never to be sent. They were just an expression of my feelings. At that time I was using a computer that had a speech synthesizer component. In addition, the letters on my monitor were oversized. It never occurred to me that my resource room classmates could see and hear everything I was writing.

My teacher finally pulled me aside and pointed this out. She explained that most girls write those thoughts in the privacy of their bedrooms, and even though she knew that wasn't possible for me, could I think about finding another way to set my thoughts down. Of course, since my classmates overheard, it eventually got back to the boy. He never spoke to me again. It hurt. I didn't understand what was going on and I blamed him. Looking back, I blame myself. It taught me a good lesson. Be careful who you talk to, what you say, and what you write about. I learned about discretion the hard way. I lost a friend.

But I kept writing. I was lucky to have an English teacher who assigned poetry often. I loved writing poems. I still do. Here's one poem about what poetry is for me:

Poetry Is Like . . .

a piece of fudge candy
a warm bath
a burning fever
a soft butterfly that flies very fast
a small, soft cat jumping around
a frisky, fat-bellied puppy
a cold, wet kitten's nose

peppermint melting in your mouth
the smell of soap
the tinkling of a lovely music box
a gentle kiss
a mousetrap suddenly closing
the anguish of unreturned love
a tear of hopelessness
the stealthy step of a tiger
the taste of strawberry ice cream
a thin line of hot, stringy pizza cheese
a refreshing dip in a swimming pool
the piercing sounds of a trumpet
the radiance of a friend's smile
the bouncing of a school bus ride
the fear of my father's cancer returning
the joy of opening Christmas presents
a hot, baked potato bursting with melted butter
the clean feeling of freshly shampooed hair
the nervousness I feel on the first day of school
the gritty feel of sand between my toes
a roasted marshmallow—brown and crispy on the
     outside, gooey on the inside
the sound of wind chimes turning in the breeze.
a soft pillow
    a whirlpool
    a bright yellow light
    a lightning bug in the sky
    a warm, sunny spring day
    a lazy, rainy summer morning
    the outside of a shiny new car

a sweet, haunting love song
    the rich feel of pink velvet
    a comfortable old feather bed
    an exciting amusement park ride
the sparks of a blazing campfire
    the steam of a hot iron
the sharp, painful stab of grief
    the bitter taste of medicine
    the suspense of an exciting book
the softness of tissue paper
a tender hug
    the growl of an enormous bear
    a cold splash of ocean water
    the sting of harsh words

And here's a "found" poem. Each line is a quotation from a *Time* magazine article by George Will about his son and baseball. I rearranged them to express my own thoughts. This was a ninth-grade English class assignment as well.

A Gentleness Straight Through

A loss in one of life's lotteries.
But physical abnormalities do not
    impede vitality.
Or life's essential joys — receiving love
    and returning it.

*Some people have superior aptitudes for
    happiness.*

*We can be forgiven for shaking a fist
    at the universe.*
*But serenity is grounded in a sense of
    completeness.*
*A shadow of loneliness, an apartness
    from others*
Is inseparable from the fact of our existence.
*We are able to think and feel, to be curious and
    amused, and to yearn.*
But there is exasperation leavened by resignation.

I had several things to be resigned about at that
time. My friends, like me, were turning sixteen.
They were all talking about getting their driver's
licenses, and I couldn't. They were gaining a freedom that I long for. My parents knew it was a difficult time for me, so for my sixteenth birthday
they took me to a Club Med in the Dominican Re-
public. I had never experienced another country's
culture. I am glad I went, but it didn't turn out to
be exactly a happy event. The people in the resort,
both staff and tourists, didn't understand me or
my disability. I was the only disabled person there.
We had been assured that it would be accessible.
Some of the places were, but none of the activities
were. I basically got to watch everyone else have
fun. Most of the tourists were from South Amer-

ica. I was stared at a lot and mean things were often said in my presence, as if I couldn't understand. A woman came up to us and asked, "Why did you even bring her here?" One day, as my mom was lifting me up over a doorway, a man asked, "Isn't she awfully heavy for you?" There were times when my mom and I were out and we could have used a little assistance over those doorways and such, but many people looked away. What was supposed to be a happy experience for me turned into one of the most distressing events of my life. I sobbed many times that week.

ᴥ Chapter Nine ᴥ

In addition to people staring at me at Club Med, I was dealing with severe, chronic back pain. As I went through the growth spurt of puberty, I grew in such a way that I developed lordosis and kyphosis. Scoliosis is when your spine curves to the side. Lordosis is when your lower spine is curved toward the front, in an S-shape. Kyphosis is the curve on the top part of the S — my shoulders rolled forward. The severe, relentless pain had me in tears almost every night after a full day of sitting in my wheelchair.

In August 1993 I went to A.I. DuPont Institute for a checkup and my orthopedist, Dr. Miller, said I definitely needed corrective surgery. He recommended a spinal fusion with a rod. There would be two incisions. One on my abdomen and one on my back the length of my spine. My entire spine would be fused so that the vertebrae would heal together into one long bone. A permanent rod would be implanted to hold my spine straight while my back healed. Afterward, my back would no longer bend. Following the surgery I would be in the Intensive Care Unit for a day or so, on a respirator and heavily sedated. This was serious surgery.

I was impressed with what Mom did. She stayed out of it. She left it between Dr. Miller and me. I said yes because I was in so much pain the suggestion of surgery didn't even phase me. I had no idea what lay ahead for me.

We liked and trusted Dr. Miller immensely, but for such an invasive surgery we felt a second opinion was necessary. The second doctor concurred. The first available surgery opening was the first week of December. My family didn't want to have it done just before Christmas, so they scheduled it for January 26, at the close of the school semester. That was probably a mistake. I was so scared. Forget about learning anything in school.

I tried to comfort myself by thinking about the last time I'd had surgery. I knew my fears about anesthesia were unfounded, yet I wrote this essay that September, when I was in tenth grade.

General anesthesia has always frightened me. So, in 1991 when my doctor told me that I needed another surgery I cried tears of devastation. I was not afraid of the knives cutting me or of the painful leg splints that would follow surgery. My fear, which made my muscles rigid and my mind whirl, was that I would die from anesthesia. I would disappear into a black hole and never wake up.

The day before surgery, as usual, I could not eat or drink past midnight to avoid getting sick to my stomach in the operating room. When someone tells you that you cannot eat or drink, food becomes an obsession. I began to taste food in my imagination!

I waited at home all morning for a phone call that would tell me when to arrive at the hospital. The telephone became my enemy. It seemed to have control over the rest of my life, as far as I was concerned. Each ring made me jerk like a bag of Mexican jumping beans. Hours crawled by until the fateful ring came at one in the afternoon.

I went to the hospital and waited some more in the holding room. The nurses offered me some medicine to make me sleepy but I knew from previous surgeries that it tasted awful. It was a thick, white, bitter liquid. I refused it. That meant that I would have to be brave enough to experience all the proceedings that would lead me to the operating room. It was hard to do.

Saying good-bye to my parents was terrifying. I thought I would never see them again. My mother told me later that my eyes were as big as saucers. The orderly wheeled me down an endless hallway toward double doors that hid the black hole of death. When they swung open, I saw the color green, bright lights, shiny instruments, and masked aliens. I was put on a cold, rock-hard table. When I looked up, I saw a mask coming toward my face.

"No! No! I don't want it! I don't want it!"

The next thing I realized was the sensation of sharp pain as I woke up.

I was alive!

No matter how hard I tried, or how much I wrote about my feelings, I still believed that this next surgery would result in my death from anesthesia. For a few weeks in December I donated my own blood to be used during surgery. We had been told by the doctor that I was going to need several transfusions and they recommended collecting my own blood. I donated four units, but as it turned out I ended up needing a total of eight. Actually, donating the blood wasn't too bad. I got dizzy only one time. Although I didn't enjoy people playing the role of vampire and taking my blood, I didn't dread it, either.

I usually adore Christmas. That year it was not enjoyable because I was totally convinced that it was my last Christmas. I really, really believed it. I wrote this poem days before the holiday:

Starting the Countdown

(Written in tenth grade)

Scared. So scared.
The rod will either "make it — or break it"
    for me.
They say it will help.
What if the pain doesn't get better?
Then I'm stuck with a rod in my back.
For the rest of my life
For no reason.

On the other hand, what if it does work?
No more pain.
That will feel almost strange.
I've had pain for so long.
It's like my CP — I just live with it.
But, with my CP, I don't constantly think
    about it.

The pain is unrelenting.
It insists that I think about it.

Kind people don't really help by reminding me
    about my surgery.
"Have you heard any more about your
    surgery?"
"When is it?"
"Are you scared?"
What am I supposed to do? Not answer?
I feel better when I talk about it, I guess.
But as it draws closer I feel myself trying to
    forget it.
Boy, it was so easy when it was months
    away!

"I wish Christmas would never come."
I said that! And I can't believe I said that!
It is my favorite holiday!
My fear has begun to wrap Christmas in an ugly
    wrapping paper.
I resent that.
Dad came in and gave me an early Christmas
    gift, in a way,
He shared some of his fears about his cancer
    returning.
And his fears about his surgeries and his
    radiation.
He said he knows how I feel.
That made me feel important that he could share
    those feelings with me.

I hope it's over with soon.
Yet, at the same time, I don't want it to
   come.
I am so scared.

I began to get so scared that I just shut down. I had trouble concentrating in school. I was unable to do homework. In fact, two weeks prior to the surgery, I began to have insomnia. My doctor gave me sleeping pills. Mom wasn't getting much sleep during this time, either. She was worried about me because I was so scared. I had nightmares about my family sitting around without me the next holiday season.

January 1994 was when the "winter from hell" arrived. The day before my surgery we were warned about a huge snowstorm coming our way. A former colleague of my father invited us to stay at his house because he lived just a mile away from the hospital. John was shuttled off to our friends the Christiansens, and we drove down to Delaware when the storm started. It snowed all the way. Our friends' house was warm and welcoming. My mom ended up sleeping in my bed with me because I was so terrified of the next day. My dad and our friends stayed up and talked. I remember hearing Dad say, "Look, we will get her there even if we have to get an ambulance in here." I asked Mom why everyone was working so hard to get me to the hospital the next day. Why couldn't we just postpone the surgery? She said we couldn't do that because my blood that I had carefully collected might spoil if we had to postpone. She told me to "try to get to sleep." She always says that before surgery. I have never understood why. I am going to be going under anesthesia anyway, and I'll be sleeping then.

We got up at 4:00 A.M., having had little rest. We drove to the hospital. The roads were almost impassable from the deep snow. I got through all the preadmission jargon questions. A last-minute physical was done, and each of my extremities were checked for normal sensation. I remember going into the waiting room with my parents. My dad lifted me onto a gurney and I started to cry because I thought I would never see my parents again. Then a nurse took me away from them into the holding room. The anesthesiologist asked, "What are you upset about? Everything?" I said, "Yes." Then he asked me to calm down. That is the last thing I remember.

The surgery lasted nine and a half hours. Afterward I was taken to the ICU and placed on a respirator. The hospital allowed a parent to stay in the ICU with me. The first night after surgery, when I was settled into the ICU, my parents came in to check on me. When they saw I was still quite sedated, they decided to go on home. They remember that as soon as my mom said, "I guess we will go now," my eyes flew open and I looked at them and immediately went back to sleep. I don't remember those days in the ICU, except for a visit from my brother. I have a vague memory of him being there and Dad showing him the machines. Mom tells me I kept asking her if I was dying yet. I guess my mind used a defense mechanism called repression, because I simply can't recall any of it. My mom stayed in the ICU with me after that first night and slept in a parents' lounge nearby. Dad and John were snowbound at home.

It snowed (and iced) for most of the time that I was in the hospital. Often I was snowed in with one of my parents, while the other was home with John. Since I was too sick to advocate for myself, my parents took turns staying with me twenty-four hours a day. This was not an easy task. I wasn't sleeping comfortably during the night. I needed to be moved or adjusted constantly because I was uncomfortable. I called out literally every five to ten minutes. Since Mom is a light sleeper, she always heard me and would always get up. Like the Energizer bunny, she just kept going and going and going. Dad fared somewhat better because he sleeps soundly.

My friend Mrs. Christiansen brought a huge box of her delicious homemade cookies to the hospital. When she gave them to me, she told me that I had the option of whether to share them or not. So I shared them whenever someone was nice to me. If they were nice, they got a cookie. If they hurt me, they didn't get one. It gave me power in a situation where I had little to none.

After twenty-six days I went home, but things were not going well. I was still in pain and still not sleeping comfortably. I was asking to be readjusted as many as fifteen to sixteen times a night. This, of course, took its toll on all of us. Things only got worse. I began to have pain in my hips that was so bad that I couldn't even stand to be moved. I went back to see Dr. Miller and found out that I had developed trochantery bursitis in both hips. Bursitis is a condition where the sacs around joints get inflamed. It is excruciatingly painful. I got cortisone shots in both hips. Dr. Miller warned me that the pain would get worse before it got better. I had several recurrences of the bursitis and several treatments with shots.

Then, for some unknown reason, I began to lose control of my bladder. Another trip to Dr. Miller. After operations with general anesthesia, constipation is common. The trauma of surgery, pain medication, and irregular eating all contribute to it. It turned out that I had become so constipated that there was pressure on my bladder that interfered with voluntary control. The wound from my incision became stubborn about healing. Another trip to Dr. Miller. Then I began to have problems with an overactive gag reflex. I would occasionally gag for no obvious reason. Sometimes I would just gag until tears ran down my face. I was not in any danger. It was just a horrible annoyance that was unpredictable. It intermittently plagued me for several years until a doctor finally diagnosed it as esophagitis (an inflamed esophagus that allows acid reflux). It is easily treated with medicine. I just wish it had been diagnosed sooner.

Complications just kept cropping up. It had been predicted that I would be in the hospital for about a week and incapacitated for about a month. Maybe miss a month and a half of school. In fact, it was three months before I was able to return to school part-time. I was on homebound instruction, trying to keep up as much as possible in the midst of all these complications. Dr. Miller could only keep saying, "Sometimes these things happen. Just hang in there. It usually doesn't go this way." But, increasingly, I couldn't "hang in there." I got more and more depressed. After school was out, my parents once again sought help. We were referred to Bryn Mawr Rehabilitation Hospital. In my first interview with the admitting doctor, I fell apart completely. I simply had no more to give. I was diagnosed with clinical depression from chronic pain. An outpatient program was recommended.

For eight weeks that summer, I spent my days at Bryn Mawr Rehab Hospital. The people there were all kind. I received every kind of therapy under the sun: physical, occupational, speech, psychological, biofeedback, and aquatic. Between each therapy session, I participated in the Therapy Plus program. It provided socialization and relaxation for outpatients who had time to kill between therapies and doctor appointments. We visited, played games, listened to music, and did arts and crafts. There I learned that some people could look at me and say, "Isn't she lucky!" simply because I can talk. I was accustomed to being with people who were born with disabilities. Until then, I had not known anyone who had become disabled later in life through accident or acquired disease. Daily I saw people courageously struggling to regain functions they had always taken for granted. That was an eye-opener for me.

In Therapy Plus I met my good friend Linda Tepper, a former fashion designer who was recovering from a brain aneurysm (a burst artery). She had to relearn how to do most everything. She was like a big sister to me that summer. Linda had regained most of her hand control when I arrived. She would do things for me that I couldn't do for myself — such as helping me with lunch or moving pieces on a board game. She was wonderful and we remain in touch today. I also met a psychologist, Dr. David

Goodwin. He treated me that summer and for a while afterward. He is warm and sympathetic and he helped me emerge from my depression.

When school started in the fall I was in pretty good shape, but I gradually began to experience more and more pain again. We figured it was from sitting all day in my chair without benefit of all the therapy movement I had grown used to in the summer. One day in October my mom noticed that I was gaunt and as "white as a sheet" when I got off the bus. She called my teacher and told her not to expect me back in class until we found out what was wrong. We went to Dr. Miller's office the next morning. Dr. Miller ordered a full back X ray, because he remembered that out of all his surgeries there had once been a boy who had developed inflammation around the end of the rod. Sure enough, both of my hips were inflamed. The rod was holding my pelvis in a position that was not right for me. I needed to have more freedom of movement in my pelvic region. Surgery was recommended to remove a few inches from the lower end of the rod. This surgery was minor and would take only about forty-five minutes. It was scheduled quite quickly — for Halloween, only three days away.

Even though I couldn't wait to end this neverending pain, when I heard that the surgery was on Halloween I was upset. John had planned a big

Halloween party at our house for his friends. I was afraid that his party would have to be canceled because of me. John had been a real trouper at first. But after nine months of my continued problems and needs, he was fed up with it. I didn't blame him and I especially didn't want the party canceled. Luckily, my parents didn't cancel it. A friend stayed with me at the hospital during the party, and then Dad came and spent the night.

That second surgery solved the problem. Twenty-four hours after the surgery I could stand on my feet (leaning on someone's arm, of course). A week after the surgery I appeared in my Junior Class Variety Show, reading my poem "Lessons Learned." What a year. Let me give you that poem:

Lessons Learned

I cannot walk; I need my wheelchair.
But I met a person whose memory is no longer
*   there.*
She can walk but she doesn't know her name.
Suddenly walking doesn't mean the same.
It's all from your point of view.

My speech is slow and I stumble some.
But I met a man whose speech he has none.
A car wreck robbed him of a voice for his
*   thoughts.*

To him, my slowness means naught.
It's all from your point of view.

I cannot write, so I must type.
But typing can serve my needs.
I met a doctor, just graduated, who can no
   longer type or read.
A brain aneurysm pushed "erase" and his
   words are mixed and tossed.
Suddenly the inability to write doesn't seem such
   a loss.
It's all from your point of view.

A doctor, a lawyer, an engineer.
A dress designer, a student, a young mother . . .
   they are all there in the rehab hospital.
All fighting back from a loss in life's lotteries.

What you have,
      What you value,
            What you can do.
It's all from your point of view.

My psychologist, Dr. Goodwin, helped me with
another difficult period in my life. I disowned my
CP. Logically, I knew I still had it, and I knew it
was a part of my life, but I didn't want it to be a
part of me. I simply was tired of it. I had been
wrestling with this for a while, and one day I was
insisting that my CP was separate from me. Dr.

109

Goodwin sharply said, "Wrong!" I was shocked. It was so out of character from his soft-spoken ways. My head was spinning. *Wait a minute!* I thought. *I don't like this!* We continued to talk about it but I was determined that my CP was not going to be a part of me! Later at home, after much introspection, I reluctantly decided that I couldn't deny it anymore. My CP is part of my life. It is part of me. I told my mom, "My CP runs my life." She replied, "Yes. You're right. It does. But just don't let it ruin your life. Don't allow the letter *i* to be in there."

Mom has a way of saying things to make them stick in my head. Maybe it was this type of comment that led to my playing with poems that build off spelling, like this one:

I — I love to be independent.

N — Nevertheless, I sometimes have to ask for help.

D — During my life as a handicapped girl, independence has become very important to me.

E — Even the smallest act of independence is precious to me.

P — Pretty often, ignorant people take away my feelings of independence by assuming I can't talk or understand.

E — Eventually, it is up to me to prove to them that I have capabilities.

N — Nothing deters me from my quest for independence.

D — Decision-making is hard for me because so many people make decisions for me about my life; other teenagers don't face that.

E — Egos are easily destroyed when you are handicapped because you have to ask for help for very personal things.

N — Non-handicapped people often don't think of inviting me places, which would let me enjoy more independence from my family.

C — Cerebral palsy makes me vulnerable in my friendships because I'm always afraid they will leave me because they would rather have a friend that can do more.

E — Everyone deserves independence.

❧ Chapter Ten ❧

After my second back surgery I began to feel good and developed a real zest for life. I wanted to try many new activities. Many sports are adaptable to some degree, and there are usually sports clubs that will help someone who is disabled. In the space of a few months I went gliding, parasailing, and snow skiing.

I visited a flying club one weekend and went up in a glider with one of the members. It was exhilarating.

Later, when we were vacationing at a lake in Virginia, I took the opportunity to try parasailing. I was strapped into a harness with a parachute attached. I sat on a special ramp on the back of a motorboat. As the boat accelerated, the wind caught the parachute and I was lifted into the air, all the while attached to a line. A big winch on the boat kept letting out my line as if I were a kite. I probably went up in the air about 150 feet. I felt like a bird, flying free. Perhaps I enjoyed it so much because I feel totally earthbound in my wheelchair. It was thrilling to be up high and to be pulled all around the lake. It was fantastic and I remember it as one of the best days of my life.

That winter I tried snow skiing at an adaptive ski program in the Pocono Mountains, about two hours from our house. I had a blast. I don't have enough balance to stand on skis so I sit in a bi-ski. The bi-ski is sort of like a sled/seat, with two skis underneath. Two volunteers accompany me. One person skis in front of me and clears the way. The other person skis behind me, holding tether lines to my bi-ski so that I won't go out of control. I steer as much as I can, by shifting my weight. The skier in the back also steers, using the tether lines. I love the feeling of speed as we zip down the slopes. The bi-ski fits right on the ski lift. We ride back to the top and make as many runs as we can, until I get too cold or my volunteer skiers give out!

I cannot adequately explain how important it is for me to try new, adventurous activities. Just like when I rode the amusement park rides with my dad, I love speed, spinning, and heights. My mom once read that most people with cerebral palsy are afraid of speed or abrupt movements. I guess I'm an exception to that rule. It makes me feel capable to accomplish different activities. Plus, it is fun! My friend Donna Jo Napoli called me "intrepid" because I like to do a lot of things able-bodied people fear. And I suppose that may be part of my motive in taking risks. Maybe it allows me a bit of one-upmanship, in my mind. I recently tried sailing in the Chesapeake Bay in a sailboat that was adapted for people in wheelchairs. It was nice, but I don't think I cared for it enough to do it again. My next goal is to try scuba diving. I can't swim by myself, but I am told that with the proper equipment and help from divers I might be able to do it. I was offered a chance to go skydiving while strapped to a person's back. My parents said it was my decision, but I said no. For now, anyway.

In my senior year, my dad took early retirement from his job. He and his company were no longer getting along, and they were downsizing so they offered him an early retirement package. However, for me, a personal event was overshadowing everything else. Our school district has a contracted program that allows kids in a local drug and alcohol rehab center to attend classes in our high school. Several of those kids rode on my bus to school. One of them stands out in my memories. He was from another town a few hours away. I fell head over heels in love with him. After the disastrous letter-writing experience of ninth grade, no way was I going to allow him to know it. It was not easy getting on board the bus each morning and pretending to just be friends, when I actually wanted to date him and have him like me the same way. I learned that he had a problem with alcohol. I admired him for being open about it. I saw firsthand that it was tough. It made me realize that being physically or mentally normal didn't offer any guarantees. There are hidden problems that can be devastating, such as the one he was fighting.

My happiest memory of him is when I told him on the bus one day that I have cerebral palsy. His response was unlike any I had ever gotten from a peer . . . especially a boy. He replied, "I don't know what that is. Would you please explain it to me?" He stayed in our area for four and a half months and then he returned home. I was heartbroken, even though I was pleased that he had managed to get "clean" from alcohol. I missed seeing him in the mornings. His own experiences made him much more mature and sensitive to my feelings, a rarity among people my own age. I wrote and invited him to my senior prom. He wrote back declining, because another girl had already invited him. He signed off, "Keep in touch. I would like to have a friend like you." That was a nice thing to say, but unfortunately I took it literally. I didn't realize then that we would both get busy with our own lives and go separate ways. I mean, I knew it, but I guess I hoped we would stay in touch. I wrote two more letters and I was crushed when there were no more replies. My mom said it was probably his way of breaking ties. I often wonder about this boy and hope that he is doing well today. Looking back over the boys I've been interested in over the years, I realize that silence is always the way they said good-bye. I don't have enough experience to know if that is usually the case between girls and boys, or if it is because I am disabled and they don't know how to handle it. In either case, I believe straightforward communication is always better than rejection by ignoring.

In high school I watched kids pair off into couples. That was hard. I very badly wanted, and still want, a boyfriend. Just to have someone to love, and to be loved back. And to go out on dates and do all the normal stuff that girls my age do. Yes, I also think about sex and what that must be like. But that is for the future. I would never have sex with someone just for the sake of having sex. It would have to be in a deep, adult relationship. I would be happy right now to have someone want to hold my hand, kiss me, and tell me I am pretty. I have terrible doubts at times whether someone will ever want to have a sexual relationship with me. I fear society's stereotype that disabled people are nonsexual will get in the way.

But, while I haven't had a sexual relationship, I have certainly had caring relationships with people outside my family. One was with Jimmy, my friend who had muscular dystrophy. After all of my experiences with the death of family members, I thought I could deal with death. I found it was completely different when it was a close friend. Jimmy died during my senior year. Everyone who knew Jimmy had been expecting his death, because we knew his disease was terminal. Each school year we watched him slowly decline physically, and sometimes he would talk about it. We watched him go through all the psychological stages: anger, denial, depression. Yet, in spite of it all, he never gave up. He studied hard and talked about what he wanted to do after high school. He was interested in art and marine biology, especially sharks. The last time I saw Jimmy he looked sad. He died in his sleep at home, on November 21, 1995. My teacher called and told me. I was devastated. I couldn't sleep that night and the next day at school was horrendous. It was especially hard for my other classmate who had muscular dystrophy. She tried to distance herself from it all, and that made me mad because I thought she was distancing herself from Jimmy. I even remember getting angry at a friend for laughing about something. I guess I thought if he was laughing, he didn't care about Jimmy. That was unusual for me. I generally think of laughter as medicine for the soul. I try to laugh even in the worst of times. But that day I simply couldn't. Fortunately, the school brought in a social worker for us to talk with, and just telling her how I felt helped me. Sometimes it just isn't fair what happens to people. It just isn't. I needed to have someone acknowledge that before I could accept Jimmy's death.

Jimmy was a great person. Knowing him and watching his struggle with muscular dystrophy is part of the reason I decided to become a social worker someday. I want to work with disabled children, and especially to help terminally ill children. Months later, after another tragic death of a schoolmate, I felt compelled to write the following:

E-mail to Heaven

(via the Heaven Wide Web)

To: http://hww.jim.com
— Hey, Jim! How is it up there? We all miss you, but I bet you are happier now. Or, are you?
— Hey, Shel. Yeah, things got very hard for me

at the end.

— I know. It was hard for me to watch you decline.

— I am happier now. My grandmother was right! I'm playing football with my great-great-grandfather! It feels good to be out of that wheelchair and to be strong and running again.

— Are you an angel, or an A-I-T (angel-in-training)?

— I haven't become a full-fledged angel yet, but I'm hoping to get my wings soon!

— What do you have to do to get your wings?

— Watch over someone with muscular dystrophy, just like I had.

— How?

— Oh, sometimes I sit with him at night when he's scared. I try to comfort him.

— Did dying hurt, Jim?

— Not really, Shel. I died in my sleep, as you know. I hurt before I died, though.

— Have you seen Mindy up there yet?

— No. She's still in Orientation.

— Did you see her die?

— Yes. It was very, very sad. I wanted to stop the fire, but of course I couldn't. I don't have that kind of power.

— Why would God let that happen, Jim? Is there a God? Have you met him?

— I'm not sure, Shel. People on Earth say there is. The angels are pretty much divided on the issue. Some say we are here in Heaven because there is a God. Other angels say there isn't and this is just the second level of existence.
— Was there a tunnel and a bright light, like people who have near-death experiences talk about?
— No. Not for me. An angel came down and floated with me up here to Heaven. Then we had to wait hours at the gate until someone processed me in. Honestly! They've been running this operation for years and you'd think they would have a faster check-in!
— Do you have any regrets, Jim?
— Yes. I wish I could have gone to art school. Maybe even have gotten married and had children. My life was just too darn short.
— Do I have an angel comforting me?
— Shel, I can't tell you that. But, I notice you put a picture of two angels over your bed. That means you must believe you do.
— I think so. There are times when I feel like I'm getting a comfort, or a strength, and I don't know where it is coming from. I just feel strong. Other times I don't have it, and I feel very, very low. Usually those are the times when I wish I weren't handicapped.

— I know how that feels.
— You don't have muscular dystrophy now, right?
— No. You won't have CP up here, Shel.
— I don't want to have to die to get rid of it, Jim!
— I didn't either. I kept hoping for a cure. But, trust me, Shel — I'm at peace with this.
— Well, Jim. I've got to sign off for now. I'm glad to hear that you are happy. Keep an eye out for Mindy! E-mail me sometime.
— I can't, Shel. You can initate contact. I can't.

❧ Chapter Eleven ❧

Like other high school seniors, in the fall of my senior year I started looking for colleges to attend. The SATs were too long and laborious for me to take verbally, plus I would have completely blown the math portion. My learning disabilities really make math difficult. I had to find a college that would accept me on a provisional basis. The community college would have accepted me, but I had decided that I didn't want to go there. It is a good school and I had nothing against it. I just wanted to be different. Most of my friends from the resource room were attending the community college. It is probably obvious by now that I have an adventurous streak. I wanted to try someplace new, and that is why I elected to attend Cabrini College.

My senior year was exciting and busy, but I continued to find time to write. I experimented with different forms of poetry. I wrote more pantoums, like this one:

Beaches

Golden sand. Balmy ocean winds.
Cool waves skipping to the shore.
Rough boardwalk that splinters the feet.
Rainbow umbrellas growing in the sand.

Cool waves skipping to the shore.
Salt water kissing people's lips.
Rainbow umbrellas growing in the sand.
Fountains of giggles erupting from children.

Salt water kissing people's lips.
Aromas — hot dogs, soft pretzels, suntan lotion.
Fountains of giggles erupting from children.
Seashells buried in the sand.

Aromas — hot dogs, soft pretzels, suntan lotion.
Crabs dancing sideways in fright.
Seashells buried in the sand.
Red shoulders. People wincing in pain.

And I wrote more "found" poems, like this one done as an English assignment, where the quotations are from Nadine Gordimer's book *My Son's Story*:

Comrades in Battle

"Nothing is simple in a life" marked by disability
    or measured by color of skin.
Each day we must get up and face battle again.
The ignorance of prejudice makes us "vulner-
    able — open, like a wound."
We must fight the "idea of oneself" based on
    what others assume.
"The humble and submissive place in society
    allotted" our kind
Makes us cry, "Equality!" Our Declaration of
    Independence is unsigned.
We must do what "enables us to keep our self-
    respect."
Not what is deemed by others to be politically
    correct.
Are we "happy for battle?"
Absolutely NO!
But, "circumstances bring out our abilities"
And make us grow.

I reveled in prose poems:

My Faceless Enemy

Society says we should "face" our problems. I think it is interesting that society tries to give problems a face, or facial features:

Face-to-face . . . A face-off . . . Face the facts . . . In your face! . . . Nose to nose . . . An eye for an eye . . . Don't give me any lip! . . . Turn the other cheek . . . An about-face . . . and (worst of all) . . . The faceless enemy.

I have an enemy. My enemy used to be absent from my dreams. I simply was not handicapped. Lately, however, I have been confronting it, challenging it, and verbally wrestling with it at night.

My enemy has shown itself in my dreams to be a pink scar. It floats. It has no face, but it talks to me. I threaten it. I say, "I'll smack you across the mouth!" It says, "I don't have a mouth!" Everything I say, it comes back to me with a retort. It is quite sassy. I tell it, "Shut up!"

It has said to me, "How about I give you a break tonight?" Meaning, it would go away. I answered, "How about you give me a break for the rest of my life?" It smugly replied, "I can't do that." It never gets tired of me, or tired of tormenting me. I am tired of it, however.

It has no compassion for me, or for anyone else. It does not ever think, Shelley's mother must be tired of dressing her. It leaves that to me.

Once it announced to me in a dream, "You know how you see a psychologist about me? Well, I am seeing a psychologist about YOU and all the trouble you cause ME!" I responded incredulously, "Excuse me???? I think it's the other way around!" Now, what kind of trouble could I be causing it? Unless it is the fact that I never give up and I will never let it rule me.

I'd love to poke my enemy's eyes out, except it has no eyes. It has no body parts so it claims mine. It determines the smallest of my gestures and the rhythm of my speech. I fight back constantly. It continues to make my life harder. It is relentless.

I cannot conquer this enemy when it appears in my dreams. I have tried to step on it. I have swatted at it. I even hid it in my dad's wallet once, but he gave it back to me. He didn't want it, either. It is very elusive. BUT, once I managed to trap it in my windowsill. It screamed bloody murder! It was caught and I was free! I dreamed that I walked into the kitchen. My mom was so surprised to see me walking! She asked, "Where's your CP?" I answered matter-of-factly, "Trapped under my windowsill." It felt good.

I wonder why my enemy has decided to confront me in my dreams? Do you suppose this is a necessary step toward adjustment? I think I will ask my psychologist. (My enemy can ask its own!)

And I won third place in Delaware County Young Poets contest with this one:

A Tree for Me

My cerebral palsy anchors me in so many ways.
It is the anchor that tugs and keeps me from
drifting toward my desires.
One of my dreams has always been to climb a
tree.
A simple wish, but one impossible.
So, at night the person I wish I could be directs
my dreams and allows me to soar in places
unknown:

I grasp at branches while my feet search and
scramble for footholds.
Higher and higher and higher.
Until I almost reach the sky!
I sit among the leaves.
They caress me.
Their touch is initimate and they murmur,
"You are free, free, free!"
The sturdy branches cradle me.
If I shed a tear it would careen downward,
skipping off leaves to a tiny muddy "plop"
below.

When I shed a tear now it mocks me as it
splatters on my tray.
Can't there be a tree out there for me?

✎ Epilogue ✎

Even though I had been writing in some form for as long as I could remember, I never called myself a writer. Throughout my school years there were always people who were suspicious about my writing. More than once my mother was pulled aside and asked quietly, "Did Shelley really write this? Or did you?" My mother was always furious when this happened. She never told me about those doubting Thomases until much later. But I guess I never got the external support I needed. Then I met Donna Jo Napoli.

Donna Jo is a local author of many books. She was looking for someone who had cerebral palsy to review an early draft of one of her manuscripts, *Song of the Magdalene*, which featured a character with CP. Donna Jo confessed that she was hesitant at first to call and ask for my help. She was afraid she might be intruding. Quite the opposite. When we finally met at a coffee shop to discuss my thoughts on her story, she guessed that I wrote. In fact, I remember her asking if I was a writer. I surprised myself by answering with a resounding "Yes!" I promised to send her some of my poetry. Several of her friends randomly entered the coffee shop and she would wave them over to our table. She introduced me to each person as, "This is Shelley. She is a writer." I had never been called that before. I was thrilled. After three hours of chatting, my mom arrived to take me home. I got in the car. "Mom! Donna Jo called me a writer!" I sent her some of my poetry. Without her continued encouragement and support, I wouldn't be writing this book. She helped me to believe in myself.

In the spring of that year I was chosen to attend a conference of the National Council on Disability in Dallas, Texas, as a member of the Student Leadership Group. Twenty-eight students were invited for the first time to join the efforts of the NCD. The NCD is an independent federal agency led by fifteen members, appointed by the President of the United States. Its purpose is to promote policies, programs, practices, and procedures that guarantee equal opportunity for all individuals with disabilities, regardless of the nature or severity of the disability; and to empower individuals with disabilities to achieve self-sufficiency, independent living, and integration into all parts of our society. There were about two hundred participants, from all over the United States. I had never been around so many disabled people in my life. I felt at home. I didn't have to think about how I looked or talked, or whether my hands were flying around. I was able to just be me, without fear of judgment. One evening at dinner, a man who happened to speak with the aid of a computer sent his sister over to tell me that he thought I was beautiful. That was the first time that had ever happened in my whole life, and it felt good.

There were speakers and workshops for three days. I participated in a Long-term Services workshop, because I knew that I will always need to manage personal care attendants. I was the only student in the workshop and the adults were helpful. I met many wonderful people. I especially enjoyed meeting Justin Dart, who is known as the Father of ADA (Americans with Disabilities Act). This was my first experience with a civil rights movement. I will never forget it. I gained self-confidence and insights into how adults with disabilities live and work. But, most of all, prior to the conference I had no idea how the ADA or the IDEA (Individuals with Disabilities Education Act) came about. I saw and met many of the people behind the movement and I learned about their huge commitment to making our society better. I also learned that even though I will promote disability rights throughout my life, I am not meant to chain my wheelchair to a blockade. I am not comfortable with that type of activism. Fortunately, the disability rights movement has room for everyone.

June 10, 1996, was a big day for me. I graduated from high school. I had ambivalent feelings about graduating. It was the end of a daily schedule that provided my contact with friends. I began to wonder if I could handle college, or if I would even like it. I was scared. Yet there were some really great things about graduating. Presents poured in! Relatives and friends traveled to attend the ceremony! Traditionally, the students in wheelchairs received their diplomas last because the lines of students move quickly. Since I was in my portable wheelchair, the president of our class pushed me onstage. I was the last student to receive a diploma . . . so I sort of had my own spotlight and my own round of applause! I was so excited that my whole body was in extension. After the ceremony my parents gave me a surprise party. When I entered and saw all the friends, neighbors, and teachers, I screamed in delight. It was great.

The summer passed and I looked forward to

college but I dreaded one thing. I knew that, just like any other college student accepted on a provisional basis, I would have to prove myself once again. When I first started Cabrini College it was recommended that I begin with one course and increase my load each semester. I followed this advice and, in doing so, I had much more time to work out my studying needs that first semester. I now take three courses each semester. In college I have finally been able to break away from that Mom-as-a-scribe study model. I still need her to do certain things, like typing my lengthy research papers. (My voice recognition computer program is too time consuming to use for such big projects.) She mostly helps me now by taping. If a class textbook is not available on tape from the library, she tapes the chapters. She reads my classmate's written notes into a tape for my review. And I, of course, have taped the class lectures. I can finally study on my own schedule. Another successful method that we have hit upon is my use of a review tape. Mom reads from the notes into a tape recorder, asks a question from the material, allows a lengthy pause, and then gives the answer. I can use this self-correcting review tape when I study for exams. I like this method. It gives me independence.

I absolutely love college. My major is human relations. I hope to someday work with disabled children in a school setting. I especially enjoy all my classes related to social work and psychology. So far the professors have all been patient and helpful. And my disability adviser, Mrs. Stephanie Bell, can always be counted on for support. Best of all, I have made the closest girlfriends I've ever had. Most of the troubling adolescent attitudes in high school that effectively excluded me are now gone. My friends are wonderful and I am certain they like me for who I am.

I have worked for the last four summers at an Easter Seals Day Camp as a Counselor-in-Training. I am in charge of storytelling and movies. Since my speech is slow, I find it easier to offer my library of taped stories and music to the different camper age groups. I also run errands for the wonderful director of the camp, Ms. Honi Carman. I run letters for parents, camp paperwork, and verbal messages to the various group counselors. In general, I do whatever I can to meet the counselors' needs. I like all parts of my job. Until I turned twenty-one it was sponsored by the Office of Employment and Training, under the Job Training Partnership Act. Now I am hired directly by Easter Seals as a part-time Assistant Counselor. I really appeiciate this opportunity. Jobs are hard to find when you have quadriplegic cerebral palsy. Plus, it allows me to pursue my career goal of working with disabled children.

I have always loved little kids for their honesty. I've had children come up to me with questions like, "How do you go to the bathroom?" "Where do you sleep?" "How do you get off that thing?" I usually laugh at these questions and answer them in an honest and direct manner. If an adult asked me these questions, I would be offended. But when a little kid asks, I know it is not meant to hurt. It is cute.

Recently a friend of mine from college was visiting me from New York. We all went to a local bike trail. She rode her bike, and I drove my wheelchair. At one point we got separated so my mom told me to wait in the shade under a tree while she went to find my friend. As I was waiting, a little boy and his mom walked past me. The little boy looked at me and asked, "Mommy! Is she in time out?" His mom chuckled and smiled at me. I was still giggling about it when my friend found me.

A lot of parents tend to pull their kids away from someone in a wheelchair, or discourage them from asking questions. I can't stand that. I would prefer parents to say to me, "Let me know if it bothers you," and then let the kids ask whatever they want. I try to put people at ease by initiating the first "hi!". Once, while waiting in my doctor's office, a couple of cute little kids climbed all over my chair, asking what "this" was and "that" was.

I cheerfully answered their questions. But I was proudest of their mother. She stood back and let her kids learn about me. If parents don't allow the questions, then all the children learn is, "Stay away from those people. Don't look at them." Once I was sitting in a store waiting for my mom when a little girl passed by and said to her grandmother, "I wish I were that tall." She was looking at me. Her grandmother quickly told her, "Sh-sh-sh!" and they kept walking. What she said was cute. The grandmother should simply have smiled at me and agreed with the little girl: "Yes. She is a tall young woman. You will be that tall someday when you are older."

Also, I can't tolerate people who want to "heal" me. I understand they think they are doing good, but I feel it is pointless. I am just being realistic. I am not going to get up out of my wheelchair and walk because a stranger puts his or her hand on my head to "heal" me. A sense of humor usually helps me in these situations, because it would do no good to get angry or cry in public. I am serious about this: Disabled people do not need strangers approaching them and wanting to "heal" them. It is embarrassing. Once when my family was in a local ice-cream parlor, a man approached my mom and asked, "Can I pray for your daughter?" Mom and I were just finishing our ice cream. Mom reluctantly said, "Sure," thinking he meant in the privacy of his home. Before we knew what was happening, this man and his whole family were kneeling around our table, with his hand on my head, loudly praying for me. It was humiliating. Fortunately, Dad had taken John out for a walk when this happened. My dad would have gone nuts.

It would be "healing" for me if the people in my everyday life would learn to accept me, accept my differences, and not add to my difficulties with their own disabling attitudes. I am lucky to have the wonderful friends and family who have supported me thus far. With their continued support, a sense of humor, air in my tires, and courage in my heart, I can only go forward.

And, by the way . . .

Mr. Rogers . . . I wrote the book!